APPRECIATING
FINE
WINES

THE NEW ACCESSIBLE
— GUIDE TO THE —
SUBTLETIES OF THE
WORLD'S FINEST WINES

RUSSIA

rranean

CHINA

CA

INDIA

Pacific Ocean

Indian Ocean

AUSTRALIA

SOUTH AFRICA

SYDNEY

AUCKLAND

NEW
ZEALAND

APPRECIATING
FINE
WINES

THE NEW ACCESSIBLE
— GUIDE TO THE —
SUBTLETIES OF THE
WORLD'S FINEST WINES

Jim Budd

APPLE

A QUINTET BOOK

Published by the Apple Press
6 Blundell Street
London N7 9BH

ISBN 1-85076-661-4

This book was designed and produced by
Quintet Publishing Limited
6 Blundell Street
London N7 9BH

Creative Director: Richard Dewing
Designer: Ian Hunt
Project Editor: Alison Bravington
Editor: Sean Connolly
Photographer: Andrew Sydenham

Typeset in Great Britain by
Central Southern Typesetters, Eastbourne
Manufactured in Singapore by Universal Pte Ltd
Printed in China by Leefung-Asco Printers Ltd.

CONTENTS

INTRODUCTION: ENJOYING WINES

W ine is made to be enjoyed. Or at least, it ought to be. Unfortunately too many people feel put off by the mystique and snobbishness that surrounds wine. "Am I enjoying this wine?" is the most important question to ask. Whether it is fashionable or chic is irrelevant. People are happy to say whether they like certain food, whether it is cabbage, tomatoes, pasta, or Cajun food. It should be the same with wine. Yet many people are frightened to say whether they like a wine or not. "I know nothing about wine," they say.

If this book gives you the confidence to try unusual and unfamiliar wines and rely on your own judgment to decide whether you like a wine or not, it will have succeeded.

The most important name on a bottle of wine is that of the person who made it. Famous names such as Champagne, Chablis, and Chianti can be great or a terrible and often expensive disappointment. A good producer is the best guarantee of quality. It is their names that are worth remembering.

Most wine books are Eurocentric; starting from Europe and working outward. I have chosen to start from California and travel east around the world via Europe and then by way of South Africa and Australasia to finish in Latin America.

With the explosion of good wines from around the world, there is no way that a book of this size can be comprehensive. I can only hope to give a flavor of what is happening. Readers wanting more detailed information should turn to the books section in the appendices.

I would like to thank the following organizations for their assistance: The Australian Wine Bureau, The Austrian Wine Information Service, The Champagne Bureau, Italian Trade Center, The German Wine Information, New Zealand Wine Guild, Sopexa, The Wine Institute of California, Wines of Canada, Wines of Chile, Wines of South Africa, and Wines of Spain.

1
ENJOYING AND DEMYSTIFYING WINE

WINE AS A NATURAL DRINK

Wine is a very natural drink. It is simply fermented grape juice: the naturally produced sugars in grapes are changed by the action of yeasts into alcohol. No one knows when wine was first drunk but it was hundreds of years before Christ's birth and somewhere in the Middle East. Certainly wine was an important part of Ancient Egyptian and Greek civilizations. It was the Greeks who spread its use around the Mediterranean.

Throughout history, especially in the countries that border the Mediterranean it has been an everyday drink—much safer, until this century, than drinking water. However, as wine is one of the relatively few agricultural products that can improve with age, it is more than a simple drink. Just like human beings, as wine ages it changes its character. Red wine changes from being bright purple when young to a plummy red and then to a brown brickiness. Aromas change from fresh fruit to often more gamy, earthy smells. With the color of white wine it is the reverse: becoming darker with age.

The great thing about wine is to enjoy it at whatever level you want: think of it as a continuum running from simple enjoyment to advanced chemistry. This continuum runs from pulling the cork from a bottle, pouring a glass, and enjoying the wine to becoming fascinated by the chemistry of fermentation or the minutiae of different barrel woods and their effect on a wine's taste.

A GOLDEN AGE?

Because of modern technology, in particular refrigeration, and increased knowledge about the chemistry involved in making wine, we are probably living in a "Golden Age of Wine." We now have the means and knowledge to make the best wines the world has ever seen. In many parts of the wine drinking world, people are "drinking less but drinking better." The consumption of better quality wine is increasing, while the demand for thin, cheap wine is declining. How-

RIGHT *There is a great variation in the color of white wines. From left to right: Château de Berbec, Chardonnay, and Soave.*

ever, there is a danger that modern technology allied with market pressures is producing increasingly standardized wines—clean, safe but boring—that taste the same whether they come from North America, Europe, or Australasia. One reason wine is enjoyable is that it ought to offer many different flavors.

WINE AND HEALTH: WINE IS GOOD FOR YOU

There is increasing medical evidence to show that regular, moderate consumption of wine is good for you. Because wine makes you feel relaxed, it helps to reduce the stresses of modern life. More than that, there are studies that show that red wine can reduce the possibility of heart attacks. One study, which became known as the French Paradox, showed that people living around Toulouse had markedly fewer heart attacks despite having a rich diet that was high in animal fat. However, they regularly drank red wine with their meals and the study suggested that it was this that was helping to reduce heart attacks.

Most wine is drunk with food and so the alcohol is absorbed more slowly. This probably helps to reduce any harmful effects of the alcohol in wine. If a few glasses of wine a day are good for you, occasional heavy binges of wine, beer, or liquor are unlikely to do your health any good at all.

CHOOSING AND BUYING WINE

The range of wine available varies greatly from country to country. If you live in France, the local supermarket or grocery store will only stock French wine. This will be the same in Italy or Spain. However across the Channel in Britain or even across the Atlantic, wine drinkers have a huge choice. Liquor stores and many supermarkets have wines from over twenty different international sources: from Argentina, Australia, Bulgaria, California, Chile, France, Italy, Mexico, New Zealand, and Spain.

BELOW *Many liquor stores and some supermarkets stock a choice of wines from many different countries, giving the wine drinker a huge choice.*

BUYING WINE—SUPERMARKET OR INDEPENDENT?

Is it better to buy wine from a supermarket, a national wine merchant chain, or from an independent wine merchant or liquor store? The answer to a large extent depends upon what sort of wine you want to buy. For most everyday wines, buying in the local supermarket or national outlet chain is probably the easiest and cheapest option. Such is the competition between individual supermarkets and between them and the national chains that these stores have a good selection of wine at competitive prices. Because the big stores buy large volumes, the small independent merchant cannot match these prices.

If you want advice about buying some special bottles of wine, such as Vintage Ports or expensive Bordeaux or Burgundy, then the best place to go is the independent merchant. They should have a bigger selection and, because these are small volume sales, their prices may well not be higher than a supermarket. Some independent merchants specialize in particular types of wine, either from a particular area or country or in old vintages of classic wines. If on your birthday, you want a bottle from your birth year the only place to go is to a specialist merchant. Nowadays nearly everyone provides mail-order or home delivery.

BUYING DIRECT

The best and most interesting way of buying wine is to buy it at the vineyard from the people who made it. Obviously, especially for those living in a non-winemaking country, this is often not possible but visiting wineries and talking to winemakers is the quickest way to learn about wine. Also if you have met the person who made the wine and seen where the grapes were grown, then the wine in your glass seems much more meaningful. It has memories for you. Good wine producers are often fascinating people. Like people and their dogs, wine tends to reflect the personality of the person who made it. Invariably if I meet a miserable winemaker, his or her wines will be miserable and joyless too!

Many of the world's major vineyards, such as the Napa Valley, those in Australia, and many French areas, are now well set up for wine tourism, which is increasingly big business. Although it can be worthwhile to visit large companies such as Mondavi in the Napa Valley or Moët et Chandon (both in Champagne and the Napa Valley), it is often more interesting to visit small producers. Large organizations have professional guides and frequently well organized tours, whereas with a small producer you may well meet the person who grew the grapes and made the wine.

Generally there is no need to book visits to large organizations, which are well set up to receive visitors. However, for small producers, it is best to phone in advance; otherwise if you turn up unannounced you may well find that there is no one around to see you. Remember that the small producer probably has to do everything from pruning the vines, making the wines to receiving visitors. It is not fair to expect a busy producer to spend an hour or two with you, if at the end of the visit you don't buy any wine or just a single bottle.

ABOVE *A roadside sign in Cahors, France.*

ABOVE *A roadside sign in Maury, Roussillon (France).*

ABOVE *Randall Grahm's tasting room at Bonny Doon, California.*

ABOVE *Wine tourism is big business in California—the gardens at Domaine Chandon, Napa Valley.*

Don't feel embarrassed about spitting wine out on these visits. If you don't do so your judgment can easily become clouded after a few wines. However, if the producer digs out a special bottle at the end of the tasting, it would be rude and a shame to spit this out. Do what the French do— *crachez en revers*—meaning spit backward and down your throat!

VINTAGE GUIDES

We all like easy answers. Vintage charts appear to give easy information about what are the good years, which are average and which to avoid. The problem is that it is never as simple as it seems. Even in very difficult years a good winemaker will make drinkable wine and, even in very favorable years, the lazy and incompetent will louse up. Vintage charts are very broad generalizations: they are rough guides at best. At worst the assessments are plucked out of thin air and are quite meaningless. If you can, it is better to learn the names of reliable producers.

Also quite frequently the reputation of a vintage is not fixed; like clothes fashions it changes. Lesser rated vintages give consumers not blessed with large bank balances the chance to try world famous names like Château Mouton-Rothschild and Margaux because the wines are much cheaper than the fashionable years.

BUYING *EN PRIMEUR*

En primeur means that the consumer pays for the wine before it has been bottled. Transport and taxes will be paid later when the wine has been bottled and is ready to be shipped. The idea is that by buying early you will get the best price and have the chance to purchase wines that will be rare and difficult to buy in later years.

Certainly it is a good way of improving the cash flow of both producers and merchants but it is much less certain that it really benefits the consumer. Essentially it means that the consumer pays the cost of maturing their wines; a charge that in the past was borne by the producer and merchant. Only by buying the few top Bordeaux wines such as Latour, Lafite, Mouton-Rothschild, Cheval Blanc, and Pétrus can you be sure of not losing money. Millionaires wanting every vintage of one of these châteaux should buy *en primeur*.

En primeur buying existed for Bordeaux and Port for many years but only started becoming widely practiced and modish in the early 1970's. Since then it has tended to go through cycles of boom and bust, depending on the quality of the latest vintage and the state of the world economy. The worst bust came at the beginning of the 1990s and the market is only now beginning to recover.

LEFT *Vintage charts give only a rough guide to which are the good years, which are average and which to avoid.*

The general introduction of glass bottles during the eighteenth century completely changed the length of time that wine could be kept. Prior to this wine had to be drunk quickly, usually during the year in which it was made. This was because it was stored either in animal skins or in wooden barrels. The younger the wine, the more expensive it was. Wines sold after Christmas were cheaper because there was a much greater chance that they were becoming sharp and turning to vinegar. The use of bottles and corks meant that wine could be kept and that it could improve in bottle.

There is now the beginnings of a new packaging and sealing revolution going on. Tetrapaks, cans, screwtops, and plastic corks are now available, so we no longer have to rely on corks. But what is wrong with corks, which make that lovely pop when pulled from the bottle? Unfortunately, cork has three disadvantages. A diseased or faulty cork can make wine taste horrid (see Wine Faults, page 19), and you have to get it out of the bottle to get at the wine. This is not difficult if you have a decent corkscrew but it can present problems. Also, bottles have to be laid on their side to stop the cork drying out.

ABOVE *Cork harvest in Portugal underway. The bark is cut off in large strips.*

Some wines, especially at the cheaper end, are now using plastic corks. Although the cork still has to be pulled, importantly there is no chance of this neutral "cork" tainting the wine. One slight problem is that a plastic cork cannot be pushed back into the bottle but it is better to reseal using a plastic stopper anyway.

Screwtops are a very practical alternative to cork, especially for picnics and self-service restaurants. Bottles are easily opened and it is claimed that wine can be kept in them for up to fifteen years. They are widely used on airplanes and nobody objects.

Tetrapaks, which have long been used for fruit juice, are now being used for wine. As there is no air inside and the packaging is airtight, wine keeps well. They stack well and don't take up much room in the refrigerator. Unfortunately, serving is problematic. They can be messy to open, especially if you cut too much of the top of the packet off. Once opened, it is probably best to pour the wine into a decanter or pitcher for serving. However, some Tetrapaks now have a slide top that is easy to open and can be resealed.

ABOVE *Screwtops may lack the magic of the cork, but they are practical and easy to use.*

Cans are also practical, especially for picnics and trips but, as few cans of wine on the market hold more than 25cls (8.4 fl.oz.) they tend to be an expensive way of buying wine.

Wineboxes, whose plastic insides collapse down as the wine is drawn off, are practical for parties. Unfortunately, because there is a slight leakage of air round the spigot, which occurs even before you open your box, the wine does not keep fresh for very long. Also, as the wine gets lower in the box especially once below the level of the spigot, air is let in and the wine needs to be finished up quickly.

It is difficult to detect any difference in taste between the same wine kept in different packagings. My limited experience suggests that wine in screwtops, Tetrapaks, and cans tastes brighter and fresher than from bottles with a traditional cork.

ABOVE *Wine keeps well in Tetrapaks, and is easy to store.*

Sadly, change is being held up by the wine trade's conservatism and consumers' attachment to the traditional ceremony involved in pulling the cork from the bottle. Unfortunately, all the new types of containers and fastenings suffer from the Catch-22 of poor image: because different packaging lacks cachet only low quality wine is used, which reinforces the already poor image. As over 80 percent of all wine is drunk within a year of being bottled, it does seem crazy to continue to use cork that can be both difficult to remove and, much worse, can turn a good wine bad.

STORING WINE

Unless you drink wine as fast at you buy it, you will soon face the problem of where to put it. The ideal place is a damp cave or cellar where the temperature is a constant 53–55°F throughout the year. The trouble is that we have spent years designing and building houses and apartments that are comfortable, warm, and dry. Try to find the coolest or darkest place as it is important to try to avoid light and heat, which spoil wine. White and sparkling wines are particularly susceptible.

It is possible to have a wine dealer to store wines for you but, of course, there is an annual charge for this. It is only worth using commercial storage if your wine is expensive and if it will not be ready for drinking for a number of years. If you do decide to have a dealer store your wine, make sure that your wine is properly insured and protected; otherwise you could lose your precious bottles if the dealer goes bankrupt.

BELOW *Light and heat spoil wine. The ideal place to store it is in a damp cave or cellar, keeping the temperature to a constant 53–55°F throughout the year.*

If wine is served too cold it may well be refreshing on a hot day but its taste and aroma will be muted. White wine needs to be sufficiently chilled to be refreshing, otherwise it will be uninteresting. Equally, wines should not be served too hot. Because of the low boiling point for alcohol, a wine that is too warm (over 70°F) becomes unstable as the alcohol starts to evaporate. It will start to smell spirity. The best thing to do is to put the bottle into an ice bucket with some cold water.

TEMPERATURE CHART

TEMPERATURE	WINE
68°F	Too hot
66°F	Too hot
62–65°F	Robust reds: Bordeaux, Cabernets from Australia, California, and Chile: Midi wines. Barolo and Amarone.
55–61°F	Most medium-bodied reds—heavier Loires, Chianti, Valpolicella, red Burgundy.
51–54°F	Best white Burgundy, top Chardonnays from Australia, California, Chile, Limoux, Oloroso sherry. Also light reds on a hot day.
44–50°F	Fino and manzanilla sherry. Top Champagne. Most white wines and rosé.
37–43°F	Sparkling wines. Any white that is not expected to taste very nice as cold will kill the flavor.
32–36°F	Too cold

BELOW *Emergency measures for cooling down wine.*

EMERGENCY MEASURES

To cool wine down quickly, you can either put it into the freezer, use an ice bucket with a mixture of water and ice, or use a cold sleeve. Twenty minutes to half an hour in a freezer should be plenty of time. Don't leave it too long otherwise the cork may well pop out.

To warm up a bottle of wine quickly, put it into the microwave. The setting should be sufficient at between 30 and 45 seconds. If a wine needs decanting do this first.

ABOVE *A wide range of corkscrews are now manufactured, some better than others. Direct to direct: top-of-the-range screwpull with foil-cutter; less expensive screwpull; "waiter's friend;" standard corkscrew; antique-style corkscrew with a brush, useful for cleaning the top of a bottle.*

ABOVE *Decanting vintage port separates it from the deposit it has thrown down while in the bottle.*

CORKSCREWS

A corkscrew should have a wide smooth screw with a sharp point but no cutting edges. The standard waiter's corkscrew, wrongly called a waiter's friend, can be difficult to use because you have to change the direction of pull halfway through the operation. They are particularly difficult to use on old bottles of wine with fragile corks. The Screwpull corkscrew and its imitators are among the best available.

DECANTING OR JUGGING WINE

A rather grand word but all it means is pouring wine from a bottle into a pitcher (jug), carafe, or a decanter. There are two reasons for decanting: making a young wine rapidly more mature by aerating it and separating an older wine from the deposit it has thrown down while it has been in bottle. Just pulling the cork will make little difference as such a small surface of wine is exposed.

For young wines, just pull the cork and pour into your pitcher etc.; the effect is even better if you can pour from a slight height, aerating the wine more. With older wines you need to be more careful, so you don't stir up the deposit. Traditionally a candle is used to light up the underside of the bottle, so you can see when the deposit starts to move in the bottle. But fluorescent lights, which are often fitted in modern kitchens under eye-level cupboards, also work effectively.

How long a wine should be jugged before it is drunk is always a difficult question. But a big, young tannic Californian Cabernet or a robust Australian Shiraz will need much more time than a delicate old wine. Young wines may well benefit from three or four hours, even over-night, in a decanter, while an elderly red shouldn't have more than half an hour otherwise it is likely to fade and die.

More reds are decanted than white. However, whites can equally well benefit, especially if they are young and closed up or the oak is dominating the fruit.

OPENING SPARKLING WINE—AN IMPORTANT HEALTH WARNING

Opening a bottle of sparkling wine can damage your sight, if you don't take care. The pressure inside a bottle of Champagne or other sparkling wine is around five atmospheres. Once released a cork can travel at over 60 mph, if you let it, and unfortunately it fits neatly into your eye! I have two friends who lost the sight of an eye because of a Champagne cork, so please *do* take care. But, with care, opening a bottle is perfectly safe.

☆ Make sure you point the bottle away from yourself and anyone standing close to you. Keep a hold of the cork as you ease off the foil and the wire cage.

☆ Hold the cork steady while you twist the bottle. If the cork will not move, *carefully* heat the neck by holding it under running hot water.

☆ Once you feel the cork beginning to move, ease it out gently.

☆ If you're successful, you won't spill a drop, but keep a glass handy to pour the first few drops into, just in case.

Never shake the bottle—unless you have just won a Grand Prix race!

GLASSES

It sounds odd but the shape of a glass does make a difference to the taste of a wine. Some glasses funnel a wine's aromas up to your nose, while others dissipate them. Smell is an important part of taste. When you have a cold and your nose is all blocked up and food doesn't taste very good, you realize how important a part smell is. Glasses should be large enough to hold enough wine without being more than half full. The bowl of the glass should come in at the top. This helps to concentrate the aromas. It is more enjoyable to drink out of a thin glass rather than a thick one, although very thin glass is unfortunately very easily broken. Some of the best wine glasses are made by Riedel.

RIGHT *The shape of a glass does make a difference to the taste of a wine. Where the bowl of the glass comes in at the top, the aromas are more concentrated.*

TASTING AND DRINKING WINE

There are three logical and consecutive stages to wine tasting: looking at the color of the wine, smelling the aroma, and, finally, the taste. When tasting, it is easiest to hold the stem of the glass.

COLOR

Look at the color. It will obviously tell you whether you are drinking red or white (or perhaps rosé). But it will tell you more. A brick-colored red is likely to be several years old. A white that is almost colorless is likely to be young. A golden colored white may be sweet or it may have been fermented and aged in oak, and it might be several years old. A very young dry white that is strangely yellow may be spoiled and oxidized; meaning that air has somehow got at the wine and aged it prematurely.

SMELL/AROMA

Raise the glass to your nose and sniff; don't agitate the glass. Now, holding the stem, rotate the glass so that the wine coats the glass. The larger area of glasses coated releases more aroma. Right-handed people naturally rotate their glass in a counterclockwise direction, whereas left-handers will go clockwise. Be careful not to rotate the glass too vigorously; otherwise you will shoot wine in all directions.

Once the wine has coated the sides, raise the glass again to your nose and sniff. How powerful is the aroma? Can you smell fruits—fresh or cooked—prunes even? Or perhaps it's a grassy or a smell of straw or hay? Or even minerally aromas? Sometimes wines can smell of chocolate, tobacco, liquorice, coffee, mushrooms, and rotting vegetables. Is there just one aroma or do different aromas fight for your attention? Do the aromas change with the length of time the wine spends in your glass? As wine gets older the aromas change. The fresh fruit smells of a young wine give away to more cooked fruit aromas, the sort associated with jam and jam making. Also, more outlandish aromas of rotting vegetables and game may develop after a few years in bottle.

It seems amazing that wine should have so many different smells (and tastes), especially as many people think that wine should only smell and taste of grapes—curiously it rarely does except for those made from the Muscat grape. Isn't identifying all these aromas being pretentious and elitist? Doubtless for some people this is true but wine is remarkably complex. Around 700 different flavor compounds have been identified. So it is no wonder that wine has a remarkable range of aromas and flavors, especially as it changes with age as well!

TASTE

Now take a good sip of wine and slosh it around your mouth. If you can take in little gasps of air through your teeth at the same time without choking, the flavor will be enhanced.

ABOVE *Wine tasting begins with examining the color.*

ABOVE *A brick-colored red will indicate a mature wine.*

ABOVE *Smell the aroma – can you smell fruits, flint, mushrooms, or perhaps jam?*

Different parts of your mouth are sensitive to different sensations. The taste buds on the tip of your tongue pick up sweetness. Those along the sides pick up acidity, while those at the back of the tongue register any bitterness, in particular tannin. This is the substance that comes from grape skins and pips. Tannin can be recognized by the fact that it makes your teeth feel furry.

As well as the flavors of wine, taste is also about "mouthfeel." Does the wine seem thin and weedy or is it round and full with a definite texture? Does the flavor change in your mouth and does the wine appear to have different layers of flavor? Also, how long does the flavor linger in your mouth after you have swallowed it? Generally the better the wine the more complex its flavors will be and the longer the flavor will linger in the finish.

People who earn their living by tasting generally add a fourth step: they *spit* the wine out rather than swallow it. If you don't do this and you are tasting, say a hundred wines, you are likely to fall over. At the very least your judgment will be impaired. But if you are tasting wine at an evening class or with a few friends, you will probably want to swallow the wine as this is very much a social occasion.

Even when you are drinking wine during a meal it is worth following these three steps, particularly smelling the wine before you taste as smell is so important to taste. Also modern winemakers make a great deal of effort to capture and preserve grape aromas in wine. However, there is no need, unless you are determined to annoy your friends, to turn this into a big performance.

WINE FAULTS

With modern winemaking technology, there are probably fewer bottles of faulty wine around than ever before. However, it will occur occasionally. Below are some of the most common faults. If a wine in a restaurant is faulty, ask to have it changed. If it is at home, take it back to where you bought it.

CORKED WINE

Unfortunately, corks are sometimes faulty. Either the cork is diseased or the chemical treatments used in cork processing have been wrongly used. Corked wine has a musty, mushroomy smell. This can vary from a faint trace to a real stink. The wine will often appear dull and lifeless, with a faintly gray hue. The taste will also be musty. Often the longer a corked wine has been open the more detectable the smell is, so in a restaurant it is still worth complaining even if you have started your second glass—particularly if it is a chilled white wine and the corky character only comes through as it warms up.

Corked wine has nothing to do with stray bits of cork floating in a glass—this is quite harmless and is caused by the corkscrew cutting off pieces when the bottle is opened. The cork can easily be fished out of the glass.

OXIDIZED

Too much oxygen kills wine but small quantities allow it to age and mature. White wines are particularly prone to oxidation, although modern technology has lessened this problem greatly. Sherry is an example of a wine that has been allowed to oxidize, so white wines which have a sherry-like smell may well be oxidized. They are also likely to be markedly yellow in color.

TOO MUCH SULFUR

Ninety-nine percent of wine has some sulfur in it. Sulfur dioxide is a vinous antiseptic, used to protect firstly the grapes and then the wine from harmful bacteria. It is also used to stop fermentation by killing off the yeasts. This is why too much sulfur can be particularly prevalent in sweet wine as the winemaker will have used it to stop the fermentation before all the sugar has been converted into alcohol.

Producers are now trying to use as little sulfur as possible and certainly sulfur levels in wine are much lower than they used to be. But you will still come across bottles with excessive sulfur. The wine will smell sulfury, eggy, and it will have a sour taste. Drinking wine with too much sulfur causes headaches.

UNCLEAN WINE

Very occasionally bottles of wines have bits of dirt floating in them. Over the years I have come across several bottles with wispy trailers of filth floating in them. This is probably because the bottle wasn't properly clean when it was filled. Don't drink wine like this, take it back to your supplier.

Once I found a mosquito in a bottle. A complaint to the wine merchant got me a fresh bottle. I drank both (first straining off the mosquito) and there was no difference in taste between them.

BELOW *Look for an informative wine list when dining out. If a restaurant prides itself on the wine selection, it will take care in presenting its list.*

VOLATILE ACIDITY

As all wine has volatile acidity, there is only a problem when there is too much and the wine starts to turn to vinegar. Wines with an excess of volatile acidity will smell and taste vinegary. It has to be said that experts often disagree whether a wine has too much volatile acidity and some wines, regarded as being among the world's best, when analyzed chemically have high levels of volatility.

PROPHETS AND WINE CRITICS

Tasting wine is very subjective. Thank goodness our tastes are not all the same. People's tastes, likes, and dislikes vary. You might imagine that when a group of "wine experts" taste a range of wines that the marks and opinions will be broadly similar. Often this is not the case. A wine will be loved by some, called "horrid" by others, and marks can vary dramatically. Nevertheless it is worth reading or listening to what wine critics think; they have the chance of tasting many different wines and so can introduce you to new wines and new winemaking areas.

Some critics and writers try to make wine tasting appear objective by giving marks on a ten-, twenty-, or hundred-point scale. It is much better to rely on your own taste and judgment rather than rush out to buy a wine because it has been given 19 out of 20 or 95 out of a 100. As Anthony Hanson says in his new book on Burgundy, "The best numbers to attach to any individually evaluated fine wine are a fax number, a telephone number, and its price, with a good address of where to find it."

There may possibly be a few people with gifted palates. But I think everyone can taste unless an illness has impaired or destroyed their sense of smell and taste. Really the most important things with tasting is practice, the chance to taste a wide range of wines and to concentrate hard when tasting. Contrary to popular suspicion, wine tasting can be hard work, partly because of the alcohol, but mainly because of the need to concentrate on what your senses are telling you about the wine in the glass.

CHOOSING WINE IN A RESTAURANT

You can tell how much a restaurant management cares about wine from how their wine list looks. A restaurant that takes pride in its wine selection will want to explain its wines to you. One that does not won't bother and will probably have a list that tells you nothing.

As well as knowing how much the bottle will cost, the customer needs to know where the wine comes from, who the producer or merchant is and what vintage it is, if it has one. Other points to look for are the number of wines by the glass and the availability of half bottles; these factors are important either for people eating on their own or for a couple who want to have a different wine with different courses. With modern wine saver devices, such as Verre du Vin and Cruover, restaurants can easily offer an imaginative range of wines by the glass without incurring wastage.

A really bad wine list often looks like this:

WHITE WINES

Chardonnay $16.99

Chablis $27.99

RED WINES

Saumur Champigny $16.99

Californian Red $19.99

St Emilion 1990/2 . . . . $22.99

The customer has no idea what they are buying as there are no producers' names. The Chardonnay might come from anywhere in the world. Just one wine has a vintage, but lists two vintages of very different quality— 1990 potentially very good, while 1992 is often dilute and disappointing. Amazingly there are many restaurants even in France whose owners have little idea about the wines they are selling and are probably happy to take whatever wines the local merchant suggests.

In contrast, here is a list from a restaurant that takes a lot of care over selecting its wines and is proud of its list.

ANJOU-SAUMUR DRY WHITE

1 **1994 Saumur Blanc Domaine de Nerleux Regis Neau**   **$15.75**
Very well made 100% Chenin Blanc. Fresh, zingy fruit—an ideal aperitif or with most first courses, fish, chicken, or veal.

2 **1994 Anjou Blanc Domaine de Sauveroy Pascal Cailleau**   **$15.75**
From the ever enthusiastic Pascal with 80% Chenin Blanc and 20% Chardonnay. Lovely ripe, floral fruit but with good balance.

3 **1992 Anjou Blanc Domaine Ogereau**   **$17.50**
While naturally without the phenomenal power of Vincent's 1990, this is beautifully made. Delightfully floral, honeyed nose, considerable fruit and finish.

4 **1994 Anjou Blanc Domaine de Montgilet Victor Lebreton**   **$17.95**
Another very attractive '94. Exotic fruit, honey, good acidity.

5 **1990 Anjou Blanc Domaine de Bablut Daviau**   **$26.75**
Low yields give rich fruit. Vinifying and aging in new oaks gives complexity.

Perhaps this goes to the other extreme and gives too much detail, but you know exactly what the choice is.

As restaurants often sell wine for three times the price they paid for it, you have the right to know what you are ordering. A restaurant can justify a high markup on wine if the wines are carefully chosen and looked after, served properly in good, clean glasses. An extensive wine list costs a lot of money to maintain. Not surprisingly those restaurants that care little about their wines often apply the biggest markup, while those who do care are much less greedy, wanting to encourage their customers to experiment by offering reasonable prices.

When the wine is brought to the table make sure it is what you ordered. Quite often vintage dates are different from those listed. This is especially true with half bottles. This may well not matter with a simple dry white or red which has just moved onto the next vintage but may well matter with an older or more expensive wine. The staff should pour a small amount for you to taste. This is done so you can check that the wine is good condition, that it is not corked for instance. It is strange how rarely waiters ask women to taste the wine, yet many of the world's best tasters are women!

Watch out for the overfilling the glasses trick! Here the attentive staff keep filling your glass up to the brim. This means that you cannot fully enjoy your wine because you cannot smell it and you can easily lose track of how much you have drunk. It also means that you get through the bottle more quickly and then feel you need to order another one. This, of course, is one reason why the staff overfill glasses in the first place.

WINE BASKETS

Pretentious restaurants often serve their more expensive bottles of red in a wine basket. The rationale, apart from impressing gullible customers, is that the pourer can thus keep any deposit from being poured into the glasses. Of course it does nothing of the kind: by pouring, whether the bottle is vertical or diagonal makes no difference, the wine and its deposit is stirred up. If a wine has a deposit, it should be decanted. If not, it can stand upright like the house wine. Wine baskets can be used most effectively for lighting fires in winter.

MATCHING WINE AND FOOD

Sunday newspapers and wine magazines like to match specific wines to particular dishes. This is doubtless fun to do and may be interesting to read about but real life is rarely like this. Wine drinkers at home tend to make broad choices—an inexpensive Italian red with pasta and pizza, a dry white with fish and a Cabernet Sauvignon with beef. Frequently it will depend upon what bottles are in the house or which labels or special offers caught the eye in the local supermarket. Often wine and food matches work OK, meaning they don't actually clash but they do not add anything to each other. It is much more rare for a wine and a dish to really marry well together.

ABOVE *Fortified Muscat works well with chocolate.*

ABOVE *Sancerre with Crottin de Chavignol: a good combination.*

Regional specialties go well with the regional wines. That robust country dish, cassoulet, goes well with the robust reds of southwest France. Oysters from Brittany are good with Muscadet produced in and around Nantes. These traditional associations of food and wine tend to take time to become established, so they are stronger in countries that have long produced wine than those that have just started during this century.

Of course there are no rules, you can drink what you like with whatever dish. But just as it is extremely rare to serve chocolate ice cream with a cheeseburger and french fries, so there are certain wine and food combinations that tend not to be used. Equally there are other wine and food combinations such as roast lamb and red Bordeaux or other Cabernet Merlot blends which are well established. Exactly like blending the flavors of different foods together, it is a question of matching the flavor of the wine with the dish, so drinking a sweet white wine with a rare steak tends not to work for a lot of people. However, it is always worth experimenting for you never know what curious combinations will actually work. Chocolate, for example, is generally a real wine killer; most sweet wines are a total failure with it. Curiously, young Beaujolais works surprisingly well. You would think it would be thin and acid but its young berry fruit blends well with the rich flavors of the chocolate. Fortified Muscat also works well.

Wine is much more difficult to match with cheese than people think. Many cheeses, particularly strong blues, wipe out red wines. So, too, does a very mature Camembert with its ammonia flavors. White wines are often a better cheese match: Sauvignon Blanc and Sancerre are good with goat's cheese and sweet wines are a good combination with blue cheese as the sweetness of the wine counterpoints with the saltiness of the cheese. If you are wanting to serve a special red wine with the cheese, then keep the cheeseboard simple, no more than two mild cheeses.

Many desserts are also difficult to match with wine. Their sweetness often hides the sweetness in a wine and raises its acidity. Sweet wines are often called dessert wines. This is mistaken as they are often better with rich patés and foie gras as well as blue cheese. Some sweet wines also match lobster, chicken, pork, and some game such as pheasant when served in rich cream sauce.

MATCHING WINE AND PEOPLE

Understandably people who are not interested in wine find someone who talks continuously about wine intensely boring. Equally, a wine enthusiast will feel frustrated and cheated if having poured a cherished bottle for friends, it is drunk without comment or any apparent enjoyment. They will probably feel that they might just as well have opened a cheap wine instead; part of the fun of sharing wine is to talk about it. Not surprisingly wine lovers soon learn to save their best wines for friends, who are interested in wine.

It is also fun to taste several different wines all from the same vintage or several wines from the same property or area but from different years.

A FEW GOOD WINE AND FOOD COMBINATIONS

FOOD	WINE
Aperitif	Manzanilla/fino sherry, Mosel Riesling, Australian Riesling, Coteaux du Layon, unoaked Sauvignon Blanc, Champagne
FIRST COURSE	
Aioli	Coteaux du Languedoc Rosé, Tavel, Soave
Foie Gras/rich paté	Coteaux du Layon, Sauternes, Tokaji
Goats Cheese Salad	Sancerre, New Zealand Sauvignon Blanc
Oysters (raw)	Gros Plant or Muscadet/Picpoul de Pinet/Chablis, unoaked Californian Chardonnay
Shellfish	Muscadet, Vinho Verde
Smoked Salmon	Fino Sherry
FISH	
Dover Sole	Best dry white affordable
Haddock	Montagny, Californian or Chilean Chardonnay
Salmon	Australian Chardonnay, Chinon
Skate with garlic chips	Corbières Blanc, Jasnières, white Rioja
MEAT/GAME	
Roast beef/steak	Cabernet Sauvignon, Chianti Riserva, Barolo
Roast lamb	Médoc/St Emilion, Madiran demi-sec/New Zealand Chenin Blanc
Pork dishes with cream sauce	Vouvray
Game	Red Burgundy, Northern Rhône, Shiraz, Barolo
Duck	As above + Alsace Pinot Gris
DESSERTS	
Strawberries	Sauternes
Chocolate dessert	Banyuls (Fr), fortified Muscat

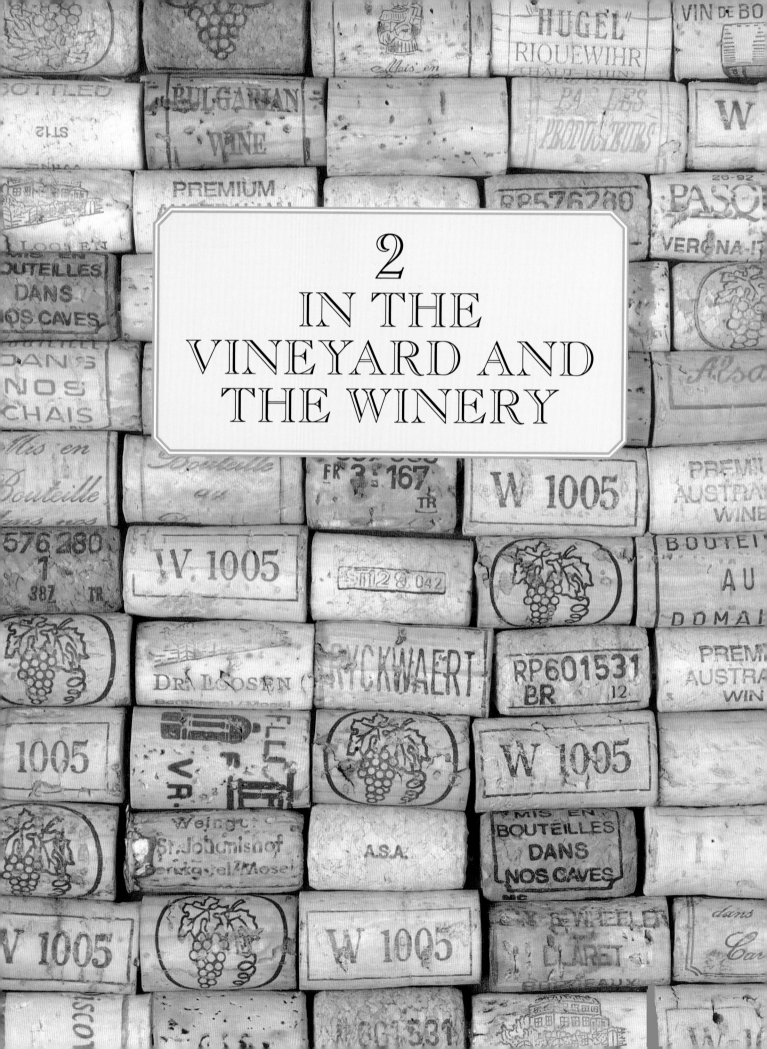

2
IN THE
VINEYARD AND
THE WINERY

The vine is a vigorous and hardy plant. This is both an advantage and a disadvantage. The good thing is that the vine will grow in very arid and rocky terrain where few, if any, other cultivatable crops will survive. The downside is that, especially in fertile ground, the vine will produce enormous quantities of fruit unless it is reined back. Unfortunately, the more bunches of grapes a vine produces, the more dilute the juice and the more insipid the resulting wine will be.

During the 1980's the emphasis was very much on the winemaker and the winery, who were frequently given star billing. This was not surprising given the increased understanding of what happens during fermentation and because of advances made in winery equipment, especially the increased use of stainless steel and the temperature-control equipment. Now the balance is shifting back to the vineyard. It is increasingly understood that no matter how many hi-tech computerized gizmos one has in the winery, it is not possible to make good or great wine unless there is good-quality fruit to work with.

ABOVE *Vines will grow in the poorest of soils—vines at Château Lastours, Corbières, France.*

THE VINEYARD

It is all-important to have good, ripe, clean grapes, which have flavor. Unripe grapes will give sharp, green-tasting wine, whereas rotten grapes unless carefully handled will put rotten flavors into your wine. The crucial decision of when to pick is the most difficult one of the year. Do you dare gamble on a few extra days' sunshine to get perfect grapes and risk the chance of rain? Or play safe and pick now?

ABOVE *Pruning in Burgundy. As well as burning the prunings the portable brazier provide warmth and cheer for the workers.*

ABOVE *Pruned vines in Touraine (France). Just a few sad twigs!*

ABOVE *Mid-April: vine shoots sprouting in California's Napa Valley.*

ABOVE *May: vines growing very rapidly. Putative branches form before flowering. Touraine, France.*

ABOVE *June: End of flowering individual grapes have formed, although they are still tiny.*

ABOVE *June: small pea-sized grapes (Roussillon, France).*

ABOVE *August: black grapes changing color, called véraison in France.*

VINEYARD YEAR CHART

There is always work to be done in the vineyard. You can't just plant vines and forget about them if you want good fruit.

MONTH	WORK
January	Pruning
February	Continue pruning
March	Finish pruning. Vine sap starts to rise and buds to swell. Vine buds begin to burst at end of month. Hope that growth doesn't start too soon as spring frosts are very damaging.
April	Bud burst continues, vine shoots grow rapidly and putative bunches form prior to flowering. Worry about cold nights—have antifrost measures ready.
May	Attach vines to trellis wires. Thin buds if required. Continue to worry about frost. Spray against mildew.
June	Flowering—hope for dry warm weather. Cold and wet will mean a poor fruit set. Spray against mildew.
July	Grapes swell and the bunches fill out. End of month cut off excess bunches.
August	Grapes change color (veraison): red varieties change from green to black, white from dull, unripe green to shiny and translucent. Get everything ready for harvest: check over picking machine, clean out press, etc. Take last-minute vacation.
September	Harvest and pray that autumnal rains arrive after the grapes have all been picked. Work 24 hour days in vineyard and winery.
October	Harvest continues, especially in northern areas of Europe.
November	Last grapes for late harvest sweet wines picked. Cut off tops of vine canes in preparation for pruning.
December	Make ice-wine in Germany and Canada. Begin pruning and identify vines that need replacing.

Most vine-growers and winemakers are individualists and practice varies from region to region and from country to country, so the chart shown here can only give an impression. Also the Southern Hemisphere will be six months in advance.

RIGHT *September: a trailer full of grapes heading for the winery (Marqués de Monistrol, Catalonia, Spain).*

FAR RIGHT *Picking Vidal grapes for the Ice Wine at the Reif Winery, Niagara-on-the-Lake, Ontario.*

PICKING BY HAND OR MACHINE?

Many of the world's wine grapes are now picked by machine. It is estimated that 75 percent of all France's vineyards are machine-picked. Early machines did crush the grapes, strip off unripe fruit, and damage the vine. Nowadays the machines are much improved and, provided they are properly set up and driven, they produce good results.

Machines certainly produce better results than an unskilled and unprincipled team of pickers, who pick everything on the vine whether it is ripe or not plus picking bunches off the ground as well as the occasional stone just because they are paid by the amount they pick. Machines are also much quicker, especially important for harvests in bad weather when it is a race against rot. Also, they can work at night, which is important in hot climates because the fruit can be picked when it is coolest. Naturally, few pickers are prepared to work through the night and, even if they are, they cannot see properly.

But machine harvesting loses the magic of the harvest—the magic of working physically hard together to bring in the year's crop of grapes. Many vineyards that hand pick use the same people year after year and there is often a big celebration at the end of the harvest. While machines are more economical, fewer people are

BELOW *Happy grape pickers. Secateurs are used to cut off the bunches. (Marqués de Monistrol, Catalonia, Spain).*

FAR RIGHT *Machine picking at the Denbies Estate, England.*

needed for the harvest and this can be an important consideration in rural areas with high unemployment. Also steep slopes can only be hand picked as machines are dangerous and will topple over. Equally small plots have to be picked by hand.

There are certain types of wine where the grapes have to be picked by hand. These are:

☆ Most sweet wines because "overripe" grapes are picked selectively as grapes do not reach this stage all at the same time, especially if there is noble rot around.

☆ Red wines that are made by the carbonic maceration method because the grapes have to be whole when they reach the fermenting vat.

☆ Top-quality wines, either red or white, where grape selection in the vineyard is very important. Increasingly, as a further quality measure, grapes destined for the world's top wines will have been sorted picked, with rotten or unripe bunches thrown away, after they have been picked. As a picking machine strips off the grapes from the stalk, this is only possible if the grapes have been hand picked.

☆ For top-quality sparkling wines, i.e. most bottle fermented ones, the grapes are picked into small containers so they remain whole until they reach the press.

NATURAL DISASTERS

BELOW *Hoar frost on vines at Clos de la Poussie, Bué, Sancerre, France.*

FAR RIGHT *Young grapes damaged by hail in July. The danger is that the damaged grapes will develop rot, affecting the others.*

Spring frosts are perhaps the most devastating natural threat grapes face. In a single night, a sharp frost can wipe out all the young, delicate buds and leave the vine grower with almost no crop. The danger months are April/May in the Northern Hemisphere and in the Southern, October and November. Sprinklers, wine machines, and burners are used to protect frost-susceptible vineyards. Generally winter frosts are not a problem as the temperature has to fall to around −13°F before damage is caused.

Hail is another perennial risk: leaves are lacerated and grapes pitted, allowing rot to develop. Fortunately hailstorms are invariably localized, so damage is restricted.

PESTS AND DISEASES

There are many different pests that affect the vine and its grapes. Vines can be attacked by rabbits who are very partial to newly planted vines, locusts, termites, and many other insects. In the past many of these pests were controlled by powerful insecticides. However, it is increasingly acknowledged that the long-term effects of using these powerful chemicals are not known. Killing off one pest may only encourage another to emerge because nature's balance has been upset. Also bombarding vines with a cocktail of chemicals probably weakens its resistance to disease, just as human beings weaken their immune systems by taking antibiotics for minor ailments.

More and more vine farmers are trying to defeat pests by managing the natural balance. Some, for instance, encourage ladybugs because they eat red spider, a pest. In parts of California growers try to encourage the leaf hoppers, which spread Pierce's Disease (see page 32), to stay in the wooded pools with their lush vegetation—which is the hoppers' natural habitat—so that they are not tempted into nearby vineyards. This is done by stopping the pools from drying out in the summer by regularly topping them up with water.

ABOVE *Phylloxera still causes grief! Grubbed up vines in California's Napa Valley waiting to be burnt.*

ABOVE *Phylloxera affecting young leaves. (Médoc, France.)*

ABOVE *One solution—grafting a new variety onto old rootstock which has developed a resistance to phylloxera.*

PESTS

Phylloxera remains the most feared pest, as any recent visitor to California's vineyards will know. Phylloxera, a native American louse with a complex life cycle, first appeared in Europe in 1863. It is thought it was carried by plants imported from North America and that the louse had survived because of the introduction of steamships which crossed the Atlantic in a shorter time than sailing ships.

Phylloxera destroys the vine's root system, killing the plant. Over the next 30 years Phylloxera came close to destroying Europe's extensive vineyards and also those of California. However, the vineyards were saved by grafting the European grape varieties (*Vitus vinifera*) onto American rootstock, which has developed a resistance to phylloxera. Phylloxera is again causing extensive damage in California because many of the vines planted in the 1970's and 1980's were on the wrong rootstock and so are not resistant to the louse.

DISEASES

EUTYPIOSE

This is a fungal disease that is spread by spores in the wind. The disease tends to attack mature vines, rotting the wood and eventually killing the vine. Because of the exposed cuts, the vine is particularly susceptible to attack during pruning. Burning the prunings and painting the cuts with an antifungal jelly prevents attack. The disease is also called dying arm.

MILDEW (DOWNY MILDEW)

This was the third American-born crisis to hit European vineyards in the last century. It first appeared in the late 1870's and is thought to have been imported on some American vines being used to graft against phylloxera. Mildew likes humid conditions and attacks vine leaves, causing the underside of the leaves to develop a white downy growth. This can lead to leaves falling off and thus a reduction in photosynthesis, the crucial process by which plants use the sun's energy.

OIDIUM (OR POWDERY MILDEW)

An American fungal disease, this first appeared in France in 1847 and was the first of the three crises to hit the European vineyards in the latter half of the nineteenth century. The disease spreads in warm weather and does not need humidity to do so. If untreated the flowering and then the growth of the berries can be affected. Oidium can be controlled by spraying with Bordeaux mixture (sulfur, lime, and water) or by more recently developed fungicides.

PIERCE'S DISEASE

This bacterial disease, found in parts of California, is spread by leaf hoppers. Once the vines have been affected, there appears to be no cure at present apart from grubbing up the vines and starting again.

TOP LEFT *A white patch of mildew developing on the underside of the vine leaf.*

TOP RIGHT *Discarded bunches of rotten grapes on the ground. The pickers have gone through the vineyard cutting off the rotten grapes before they pick the healthy ones. (Coteaux du Layon, Loire, France.)*

BOTTOM LEFT *Chenin Blanc with noble rot starting to form. The individual grapes vary widely from just ripe to over-ripe. (Coteaux du Layon, Loire, France.)*

BOTTOM RIGHT *Again, Chenin Blanc in the Coteaux du Layon, but two weeks later with further developed noble rot shrivelling up the grapes.*

ROT

Ripe or nearly ripe grapes can rapidly turn rotten in warm, wet humid conditions. Wine producers dread rain at harvest time. Not only do the grapes tend to suck up the water, diluting the juice and thus the wine, but also the fruit may well turn rotten when attacked by gray rot (in French *pourriture grise*). Rotten grapes make rotten wine, especially for red where the juice stays in contact with the skins. It is less a problem with white wines if pressed immediately and the juice is allowed to settle.

But there is also noble rot (*pourriture noble* or botrytis) and many growers welcome this. It is caused by the same bacteria as gray rot. It just depends on the weather as to which variety develops. If the weather stays damp and wet, then it will be gray rot and worried vignerons. If there are cool nights followed by misty mornings with the mist then being burned off by a warm autumnal sun, noble rot will develop and vignerons, especially those wanting to make sweet wine, will be smiling.

Noble rot eats up a grape's water content, and so concentrates the sugars. It also turns the outside of the grape a disgusting and unappetizing browny black. But however disgusting the grapes may look, the taste is good. Almost all the great sweet wines of the world, such as Sauternes, Loire Coteaux du Layon, German Trockenbeerenauslese, and Hungarian Tokaji come from vineyards planted on the sides of valleys that are prone to autumnal mists.

The last two decades of this century have seen growing doubts over the enormous growth since 1945 in the use of chemicals, fertilizers, insecticides, fungicides, and weedkillers in the vineyards. More vine farmers are cutting down on the use of chemicals and some are choosing to farm organically. This means not using any artificial fertilizers or sprays—Bordeaux mixture is usually the only spray treatment allowed.

Winemakers disagree over whether wines should be labeled organic or not. Some producers do emphasize that their wines are produced organically but many of the best-known estates using organic methods make no mention of it on their labels. They believe that it is the taste that is important.

At the furthest extreme of organics, there is also a small but growing number of people using the biodynamic system of cultivation. This is based on the theories of the Austrian Rudolf Steiner and links activities in the vineyard and winery to the cosmos. Natural treatments for the vine have first to be energized for a very specific length of time and then applied at a particular moment. It is too bad if this happens to be four o'clock in the morning! Biodynamics may appear lunatic to "city sophisticates" but is certainly no more crazy than pouring an arsenal of potentially polluting chemicals onto the land. Soil experts claim that because of the overuse of chemicals that some famous vineyards in Burgundy (and doubtless elsewhere) have less microbial life than the Sahara Desert.

There is also a realisation that a monoculture of vines, just like a monoculture of cabbages or turnips, builds up problems of disease. It is much better to keep surrounding woodlands and perhaps to have vineyards interspersed with other crops than to have an unchanging sea of vines.

RIGHT *Irrigating vines at Fetzer, Mendocino, California. Fetzer use organic methods at their Valley Oaks Estate in Hopland.*

WHY ARE THEY IMPORTANT?

Different grape varieties have very different flavors and characteristics. Some are adapted to hot climates, while others do better where it is cooler with a slower, longer growing period. Although no vine needs large quantities of water, some are better adapted to drought than others.

In countries such as France, Italy, Spain, and parts of Eastern Europe where vines have been cultivated for centuries growers have gradually discovered with varieties work best in their vineyards and climate. Sometimes, such as with the Pinot Noir in Burgundy, these are probably native wild vines that have been civilized. In the newer wine-producing countries the tendency has been to plant internationally famous varieties such as Chardonnay and Cabernet Sauvignon. Now many of these new countries are beginning to experiment with different varieties and to slowly work out which are the best varieties for their particular situation.

Until about fifteen years ago most quality wine was sold using the name of the area from which it came. Wines such as Chablis, Montrachet, Château Lafite and Châteauneuf-du-Pape are all named after places and give no indication about which grape varieties are used and whether these are single grape variety wines or blends of varieties. The question of grape varieties just was not seen as important for the consumer.

All that has changed now. For many wines the grape variety is the most important fact—put Chardonnay on the label of white wine and the chances are that it will sell. Varietal wines appeal to the new consumer, it makes wine much easier to understand. There is no need to remember a whole load of geographical names that are often virtually meaningless unless you have actually been there. It is much easier to remember that you like the taste of Sauvignon Blanc or Chardonnay and experiment with the differing flavors of a Chardonnay from New Zealand, Australia, Languedoc, the Loire Valley, Italy, Austria, and California.

ABOVE *Chardonnay. (Grand Cru, Chablis.)*

ABOVE *Chenin Blanc. (Saumur, France.)*

ABOVE *Furmint. (Tokaji, Hungary.)*

ABOVE *Gewürztraminer. (Rheinhessen, Germany.)*

SYMBOLS

dr: dry   sw: sweet   sp: can be used for sparkling   [ ]: occasionally

ALIGOTÉ (dr)

Burgundian grape that plays second role to Chardonnay. Produces lemony, quite acidic wine, the best coming from the small village of Bouzeron in the Côte Chalonnaise. It is the classic wine to use for a *kir*.

CHARDONNAY (dr/sp)

This is undoubtedly the world's most fashionable white grape. Burgundy is its home and Montrachet, Meursault, Corton-Charlemagne, and Chablis Grand Cru are the supreme (and expensive) examples. Chardonnay is popular with growers, winemakers and consumers. Styles range from fresh and floral in the Loire to blowsy, buttery, exotic oaky fruit in the hotter parts of Australia. The white grape of Champagne.

CHENIN BLANC (dr/sw/sp)

One of the world's most versatile grapes, capable of making wines from bone dry to lusciously sweet and both still and sparkling. Chenin is not as popular as it should be because care is needed both in the vineyard and winery for it to show well. Almost all the best Chenin comes from the Loire, except for a few New Zealand estates. Still the most widely planted grape in South Africa where it is called Steen.

COLOMBARD (dr)

Originally used for making Armagnac and Cognac but now increasingly used in southwest France to make crisp, lightly floral, easy drinking wine. Used to make cheap jug wine in California, also planted in South Africa.

FOLLE BLANCHE/GROS PLANT

Produces sharp, acid wines that are ideal for oysters and also for brandy production. Known as Gros Plant in Loire vineyards around Nantes.

FURMINT

This is the great grape of Hungarian Tokaji, so expect to hear more about it in the future. Susceptible to noble rot, it can produce both dry and sweet wines. Called Sipon in Slovenia.

GEWÜRZTRAMINER (dr/sw)

Because of its highly perfumed, spicy aroma, Gewürztraminer is a very easy variety to pick out. At its best in Alsace where it can be both dry or picked late to give sweet wines. It is also grown in California, Germany, Australia, and New Zealand.

ABOVE *Marsanne. (Rhône, France.)*

ABOVE *Muscat. (Hunter Valley, Australia.)*

ABOVE *Pinot Gris, late harvest. (Alsace, France.)*

GRENACHE BLANC (dr/sw)

Quite widely planted in Spain and Languedoc-Roussillon. With modern technology better wines are being produced but, so far, nothing really exciting. Best used in VDNs like Rivesaltes.

LASKI RIESLING (ALSO ITALIAN/WELSCHRIESLING) (dr [sw])

Extensively grown in northern Italy and eastern Europe, especially in the area around Lutomer (Slovenia). Usually bland and anonymous but can be good with low yields and serious winemaking.

MARSANNE (dr)

Leading white variety from the Northern Rhône, especially in white Hermitage. It gives full bodied wines that can age well. Also now being planted in Languedoc-Roussillon plus some successful plantings in Australia.

MÜLLER-THURGAU (dr/sw)

A cross between Riesling and Silvaner, this is rarely allowed to produce interesting wine. Mainly used in Germany to make high-volume wines like Liebfraumilch and Piesporter Michelsberg.

MUSCADET (dr)

Although originally from Burgundy, it is now grown almost entirely in the Loire vineyards just to the south and east of Nantes. An early ripener, Muscadet gives fairly neutral wine but is good with fish and the best can age interestingly.

MUSCAT (dr/sw/sp)

An extended family rather than a single variety, Muscat may be the oldest grape type. Easily recognizable perfumed style—tangerines, oranges, and marmalade. The wines are often sweet, frequently fortified especially from the Mediterranean and Australia. Alsace produces a dry style as increasingly do some Roussillon producers. In Italy it is widely used to make sparkling wine low in alcohol. The best known varieties are Muscat de Petits Grains and Muscat d'Alexandria. Muscat is also a table grape.

PINOT BLANC (dr/sp)

Although not a grape you would kill for, it is a good base for sparkling wines, such as Crémant d'Alsace and makes perfectly decent still wine. Called Weisserburgunder in Germany and Austria.

PINOT GRIS (dr/sw)

Produces spicy quite opulent wines, especially in Alsace and Germany, which match game dishes well. Known as Pinot Grigio in Italy, where it makes rather anonymous wines, called Beli Pinot in Slovenia and Grauburgunder and Rulander in Germany. Was called Tokay until this was banned by the European Union because of the clash with Tokaji, the famous Hungarian wine.

ABOVE *Viognier. (Rhône, France.)*

RIESLING (dr/sw/sp)

Like Chenin Blanc, this is both a very versatile and one of the great varieties. At its best in Alsace and Germany, producing wines that range from bone dry to lusciously sweet but always with a wonderful crisp acidity. The best wines age brilliantly. Australia also produces interesting examples but as yet not on par with best from Germany. Not to be confused with Laski Riesling.

ROUSSANNE (dr)

Best known for its role in Hermitage Blanc, Roussanne has been increasingly planted in Languedoc-Roussillon to improve their whites.

SAUVIGNON BLANC (dr/sw)

The aromatic variety that has followed Chardonnay around the world is generally better from cool climate vineyards. Originally the best examples came from the Central Loire. In last decade New Zealand has challenged this. It is rare for Sauvignon to have the complexity of Chardonnay. Grassy, nettly, grapefruit in cool climates, in warmer climes it is often blandly exotic. However, it is an important constituent part of Graves, Bordeaux's finest dry white wine, and the sweet wines of Sauternes and Barsac.

SEMILLON (dr/sw/sp)

The classic white variety of Bordeaux and the essential ingredient in Graves and Sauternes with a rich opulent flavor, though inclined to waxiness. Often blended with Sauvignon. Has very good aging potential and old Semillon from Australia's Hunter Valley can be a revelation.

SYLVANER (OR SILVANER) (dr/sw)

Pleasant enough easy drinking, everyday grape in Alsace but the leading traditional quality grape in Germany's Franken region.

VERDELHO (dr)

Best known for the eponymous dry Madeira but also grown in Australia to make very interesting and flavorsome dry whites.

VIOGNIER (dr)

For much of this century Viognier, which has a characteristic aroma and flavor of apricots, has been confined to the northern Rhône Valley. An irregular cropper, it is an increasingly fashionable variety in Languedoc-Roussillon and California, where it is a much less erratic cropper. Best drunk young.

VIURA OR MACCABEO (dr)

Widely planted in northern Spain and parts of France's Midi. Generally dull grape which is at its best in Rioja.

ABOVE *Cabernet Franc. (Chinon, France.)*

ABOVE *Cabernet Sauvignon. (Mendoza, Argentina.)*

ABOVE *Carignan. (Minervois, France.)*

CHIEF RED VARIETIES

BARBERA (md)

This is widely grown in northern Italy, gives an interesting mix of deep colored sweet fruit and acidity. The wines are often easy to drink.

CABERNET FRANC (lg-md)

The Franc is King in the Loire, producing the best reds but is largely an also ran in Bordeaux, except at Château Cheval Blanc. Ripens earlier than its cousin, Cabernet Sauvignon, and produces softer, more approachable wines when young which have the potential to age. Ought to be more widely planted in New Zealand and South Africa.

CABERNET SAUVIGNON (md-rb)

The most fashionable red variety giving well-structured, tannic wines that can age well. Blackcurrant is often the most dominant flavor. Now grown around the world but originally from Bordeaux area. Often the best results come when it is blended with Merlot, which softens it down. As it ripens late, Cabernet Sauvignon can be problematic in marginal wine regions.

CARIGNAN/CARINENA (md-rb)

This is the workhorse red of the Midi and Spain. But low-yielding, old vines can produce very interesting powerful wines, so Carignan is gaining greater respect. Some new examples from California.

CINSAULT (lg-md)

Widely planted but not highly regarded in France's Midi. Tends to produce large crops of uninteresting wine, Cinsault is now often used for making rosé.

GAMAY (lg)

This is the archetypal easy drinking red, potentially at its best in the Beaujolais. Carbonic maceration is widely used to emphasize its fruitiness. It is also grown in the Loire especially Touraine and Anjou.

GRENACHE (md)

This Mediterranean grape is important in the Southern Rhône, Languedoc-Roussillon and Spain. Grenache gives soft, mouth-filling wine that tends to age quickly. Tobacco aromas are common. It is also a mainstay of vin doux naturel from Banyuls, Maury and Rivesaltes.

ABOVE *Grenache. (California, USA.)*

ABOVE *Ripe Merlot. (Graves, France.)*

MALBEC, COT, AUXERROIS (md-rb)

A markedly tannic variety and the one that made the black wine of Cahors famous. Called Malbec in Bordeaux, Auxerrois in Cahors, and Cot in the Loire. It makes some of Argentina's best wines, Malbec deserves more attention.

MERLOT (md)

Like the classic police duo, Merlot often plays the soft, amenable role to Cabernet Sauvignon's hard man. Now planted worldwide, except cool climates where its early budding and fragility during flowering are disadvantages, its soft plummy fruit shows its very best in Pomerol—with prices to match!

MOURVÈDRE (rb)

Mediterranean variety of high quality but can be difficult to get ripe. Generally needs to be close to the sea and at its best in Bandol (Provence).

NEBBIOLO (rb)

Possibly the greatest grape of Italy, its home is in Piedmont where it is famous for Barolo and Barbaresco. Potentially very tannic and needing long aging, modern methods are making Nebbiolo more approachable.

PINOTAGE (md-rb)

A cross between Cinsault and Pinot Noir, this is South Africa's most distinctive variety. At its best the wines have rich plummy fruit, less attractive examples smell and taste of burnt rubber and farmyards.

PINOT MEUNIER (md)

Best known as the third grape used in the production of Champagne. Its name comes from the floury appearance of its leaves—Meunier is French for miller.

ABOVE *Ripening Nebbiolo, about a month before harvest. (Barolo, Italy.)*

ABOVE *Ripening Pinot Noir, late August. (Côte Chalonnaise, France.)*

ABOVE *Zinfandel. (Napa Valley, California, USA.)*

RIGHT *Sangiovese. (Mendoza, Argentina.)*

PINOT NOIR (lg-md)

The variety that challenges the world's winemakers: difficult to grow (rots easily) and difficult to vinify (lack of color in the skins). The grape of red Burgundy, Pinot Noir can be great but is frequently a dreadful disappointment. Good examples now coming out of New Zealand, California (Carneros) and Oregon.

SANGIOVESE (md)

This is the most important grape of Central Italy, especially Tuscany. Also becoming fashionable in California. Styles range from light, easy drinking to full bodied and needing aging as in the case of top Chiantis and super-Tuscans, often blended with Cabernet Sauvignon.

SYRAH (SHIRAZ IN AUSTRALIA) (rb)

Top-quality grape from the northern Rhône making deep colored, powerful wines. The best of these can age wonderfully. Now widely planted in the Midi and increasingly in California. As Shiraz in Australia makes some of that country's best reds.

TEMPRANILLO (md)

Spain's best native red grape and now increasingly appreciated. Also known as Cenibel and Tinto Fino, a variant of Tempranillo, is used in Ribera del Duero. It reacts well to oak and the wines can be long lived.

ZINFANDEL (md-rb)

California's most intriguing grape whose origins remain mysterious but whose quality and potential is now being recognized by some producers in its native vineyard. At its best as a red but white Zinfandel (actually a rosé) has been popular and a great commercial success.

The traditional idea is that wine is made in a picturesque cellar full of large old barrels, along with cobwebs and genial old peasant: in short a form of alchemy. Such cellars still exist but many wineries now have no more magic than a clean cheese factory. The genial old peasant has given way to a technician with a clipboard checking computer dials among shiny hi-tech equipment.

Much of the equipment in a modern winery is stainless steel, which is easy to use and to keep clean. Cleanliness is very important in winemaking if faults and poor flavors are to be avoided. There is a saying that it takes seven liters of water to make a liter of wine! This is not a modern version of the miracle of Cana but the amount needed to wash down floors, clean out the presses, vats and so on.

All recent wineries are equipped with temperature controlled vats, so that the winemaker can decide exactly what temperature the grape or wine must be. Controlling the temperature is particularly important during fermentation, which creates a lot of heat. In the most modern wineries control is by a central computer panel.

However, although the techniques and equipment are now more sophisticated, the principles of winemaking remain the same.

FERMENTATION

Grape sugars are converted by the action of yeasts to alcohol. This process is called alcoholic fermentation and will continue until either all the sugar in the grapes has been used up or the process has been stopped by cold (yeasts cannot work) adding sulfur (killing the yeasts) or by centrifuging the liquid (getting rid of them). The riper the grapes, the more sugar they will have and potentially the more powerful the wine will be. Yeasts stop working at 15.5–16 percent alcohol—perhaps they are overcome by the fumes!

ABOVE *Water running down the outside of a stainless steel vat to lower the temperature of fermentation. (Champagne, France.)*

RIGHT *An array of stainless steel fermenting and storage tanks at Cave Cooperative of St. Cyr, Saumur, France.*

ABOVE *Small oak barrel showing fermentation froth. (Coteaux du l'Aubance, Loire, France.)*

There is another type of fermentation that some wines go through called *malolactic fermentation*, often called "the malo." This changes the green malic acid, like the tart acidity in a green apple, to lactic acid—a softer, milkier acid. The malolactic normally happens after the alcoholic fermentation. All red wines have a malo as do some whites but not those which need a crisp, lemony acidity.

Cut most black grapes open and you will find that it is only their skin that is black. The flesh is white. A few varieties do have red flesh, such as Alicante Bouchet or Dornfelder, but none of them make more than pretty ordinary wine. It is therefore the methods used that distinguishes making red and white wines, since the "raw materials" are much the same. Making rosé is a mix of the two methods.

MAKING WHITE WINES

It is important to start processing white grapes as soon as possible after they have been picked, otherwise they start oxidizing and their aromatic qualities are lessened. The grapes are normally separated from their stalks. Although grape skins have natural yeasts on them and there are natural yeasts around the winery, some winemakers prefer to add artificial yeasts to give them greater control. If required, yeast is added now and then the grapes are pressed. When making sparkling wine, bunches often go straight into the press whole.

After pressing, the juice is usually allowed to settle and clarify. The juice, or *must*, is then pumped into vats to ferment. This is now usually stainless steel tanks, although top-quality whites are put into new oak barrels. Fermentation creates heat and modern refrigeration equipment allows the winemaker to control the temperature. Most whites are fermented at 63–72°F. Going above this temperature makes the wines heavy and lacking in freshness, going below tends to make all wines taste the same.

RIGHT *Bank of modern pneumatic presses at Beaulieu Vineyards, Napa, California. The presses are computer controlled and have inflatable bags inside which press the grapes very gently.*

After the end of the alcoholic fermentation and the malolactic, if this is wanted, the wine is moved (*racked*) to another tank to separate it from its lees: dead yeast cells and other debris left over from the fermentation. However, some wines such as Muscadet are kept until bottling on their lees to give additional flavor. The wine is left to mature either in tank or barrel. Then several vats will be blended together to make the final blend.

To make the wine clear, it is *fined*. Egg whites are lightly beaten, and as they sink down through the wine they take any suspended particles with them. Instead of egg whites dried, ox blood or bentonite (a type of clay) can be used. Most wines are then *filtered*, so that the wines appear really bright and free of any tartaric crystals. These crystals are natural and entirely harmless but worryingly look like cut glass, so producers play safe and remove them. However, there are some producers who refuse to filter their wines believing that filtration removes flavor from the wine as well as unwanted particles. At this point most wine is put onto the market but some top-quality wines may spend further time maturing in bottle before being released for sale.

The process is the same for *sweet wines*, except that fermentation often takes longer because the quantity of sugar slows down the action of the yeasts. Pressing is also more difficult because of the small amount of juice in very ripe grapes. The difference is that the grapes are left to become super-ripe, eventually shriveling up to become raisin-like. In some areas the grapes will be affected by noble rot. It is also possible to dry the grapes after they have been picked. French *vin de paille* and Italian *passito* are examples of this method.

MAKING RED WINES

Because the wine's color has to come from grape skins, the grapes have to stay in contact with the juice during fermentation and so the grapes are pressed at the end rather than the beginning. When the grapes arrive at the winery, they may be destemmed to separate them from the stalks. The stalks, like the pips and skin, contain tannin, which is what makes your teeth feel furry when you chew a grape pip. It is a question of how much tannin the winemaker wants. If the wine is to age some tannin is required but too much hides the fruit and makes the wine astringent.

Then, for the *classic fermentation method*, the grapes are lightly crushed to break their skins and loaded into the fermentation vats, which may be made of wood, cement, or now more usually are stainless steel. The grape skins macerate with the must during fermentation giving color, flavor, and tannins to the wine. The skins and pips naturally float to the top and form a cap. This has to be submerged back into the liquid, so that color and so on continues to be extracted. The traditional and laborious method is for people to tread the cap down. This is still done in places such as the Duoro valley in Portugal. There are specially designed machines to submerge the cap or wine from the bottom of the tank can be pumped over the cap. Or the cap can be broken up by releasing inert gas or air into the tank.

RIGHT *Cap of grape skins on top of a vat of fermenting red must. (Bodegas Muga, Haro, Rioja, Spain.)*

BELOW *Foulage (the traditional method of submerging the grape skin cap) for the Hermitage wine of M. Chapoutier, Tain l'Hermitage.*

The longer the skins and pips stay in contact with the juice the deeper the color and more tannic and full-bodied the wine. If soft, fruity wine is wanted the contact time may only be three or four days. For long-lived powerful reds, it can be three weeks or more. Reds are allowed to ferment at higher temperatures than white wines. Temperatures used range from about 72°F to 93°F. Going above this temperature may spoil the wine.

After sufficient maceration, the juice is separated from the skins and pips. If necessary the free run wine finishes its fermentation and then undergoes its malo. The debris that is left behind goes to be pressed. The press wine is then kept separate as it is more tannic and bitter. However, small quantities of the press wine may well be added when the final blend is made to give the wine more body and structure.

The wine is then treated in the same way as white wine: racking, a varying period of maturation, fining, filtration, and then bottling.

Some red wines are made by *carbonic maceration*. The grapes are put into the vat whole, with conveyor belts being used so that the berries are not crushed. The vat is sealed and carbon dioxide is often added. Fermentation starts inside the individual berries, until the buildup of gas bursts the grape. Then fermentation continues in the classical way. Of course the grapes at the bottom of the vat soon burst because of the weight, so really there is always a mixture of the two methods.

Carbonic maceration emphasizes the fruit aromas and flavors, ideal for wine that is to be drunk young. This fermentation method certainly produces different flavors from the classic method with the wines often having a fruity smell of bananas.

MAKING ROSÉ

There are three ways of making rosé. One is to press the grapes immediately so that the color comes from the brief contact between the juice and the skins in the press. This method produces the palest rosé. Another method is to crush the grapes and have the juice and skins macerate for between twelve and twenty-four hours. Then the juice is separated by pressing the grapes. The third method is to run some juice off a red wine vat after a short period of maceration (up to twenty-four hours). This helps to concentrate the resulting red wine. In France this method is called *saignée* (to bleed).

Whatever the initial method used, once the juice has been separated fermentation is exactly the same as for white wines using similar temperatures. In France, except for Champagne, rosé cannot be made by blending red and white wine together. Elsewhere some cheap rosés are made this way.

MAKING SPARKLING WINES

For the best results grapes should not be too ripe nor should they be too highly flavored. Generally the best sparkling wine is made in cool climates and from varieties like Chardonnay, Pinot Noir, Pinot Blanc rather than pungent varieties like Gewürztraminer. Muscat is an exception to this with wines like Asti Spumante.

There are several ways of making sparkling wine but everyone agrees that the best results come from a second fermentation in the bottle. This used to be called *méthode champenoise* but the term is now banned, now it is sometimes called *méthode traditionelle*. This is the process used for Champagne and all the world's other top sparkling wines.

After the first fermentation has finished, nowadays usually done in tank but sometimes in barrel, the base wine is bottled with the addition of some sugar and more yeast. The bottle is then sealed. Once cork was used but now they are sealed with a crown cork. The bottles are stacked on their side, preferably in a cool cellar of the type found in Champagne, or in a temperature-controlled warehouse. The added sugar and yeasts causes fermentation to start again, producing carbon dioxide. Because the bottle is sealed, the gas cannot escape and is absorbed by the wine. On average a pressure of five to six atmospheres builds up inside the bottle. (In the early days of Champagne making during the eighteenth and early nineteenth centuries, workers in the cellars wore iron masks to protect their faces against flying glass as so many bottles exploded.)

Although the secondary fermentation will only take a maximum of eight weeks, the bottles are left undisturbed for at least nine months and often much longer. This is because the wine needs to age. During this time it will pick up yeasty or bready flavors from the dead yeast cells. This slow process is called *autolysis*. The longer the wine stays on its lees the more complex and flavorsome it will be.

RIGHT *Bottles of Champagne stored for secondary fermentation and aging in the extensive cellars of Mercier. Notice the red crown corks.*

Now there is the problem of what to do with the debris left in the bottle from the second fermentation. Traditionally the bottles were put into riddling racks and turned gradually by hand (riddling or *remuage* in French) until the cork was pointing downward and the grunge inside rested against the cork. Although some hand riddling is still done, most is done by machines with the bottles stacked into metal palettes and then inverted mechanically.

The neck of the bottle is frozen by dipping it into a freezing salt solution, the debris is fired out by the pressure inside the bottle, the bottle is topped up and recorked, this time with a "Champagne" cork. At this stage the *dosage* is added. This is a mixture of wine and sugar syrup which determines how dry or sweet the finished wine will be. Ideally the wine should then be kept for at least a further three months so that the wine and the dosage blend in properly together. Bottle fermented wines can continue to improve in bottle. This is why Champagnes that are put on the market too soon initially tasting green and acidic, may improve greatly if they are kept for six months or a year.

ABOVE *Bottle rack for hand riddling. (Bouvet Ladubay, Saumur, France.)*

ABOVE *Frozen debris and discarded crown corks from sparkling wine that has been shot out at the time of final bottling. The process is called degorgement in France. (Domaine Chandon, Napa Valley, California.)*

DEGREES OF SWEETNESS IN CHAMPAGNE

CATEGORY	OUNCES OF SUGAR PER GALLON
Extra Brut (or Brut Zero)	0.66 oz
Brut	up to 2 oz
Extra Sec (Extra Dry)	1.5–2.65 oz
Sec or Dry	2.3–4.63 oz
Demi-Sec	4.37–6.62 oz
Doux or Sweet	6.62 oz +

Inevitably bottle fermentation is an expensive process and may well not be viable if either your grapes are not that good or you need to produce a cheap sparkler. In the Charmat or *Cuvée Close* method, the secondary fermentation takes place in a large tank. This is a much cheaper and quicker method. While the results are not as good, these are perfectly good for large parties and weddings. The cheapest but least successful way is to carbonate wine in the same way that fizzy drinks are made by pumping carbon dioxide into it.

Méthode ancestrale is the oldest way of getting a sparkle into the bottle. In the olden days, because yeasts stop working during the cold of winter, wine would sometimes be bottled before its fermentation was actually finished. Then in the warm of spring, it would start again. This method is still used for some of the sparkling wines from Gaillac and Limoux.

ABOVE *Emptying and filling carboys of Vin Doux Naturel at Mas Amiel, Maury in the Roussillon, France. The wine is aged outside for a year.*

ABOVE *A cooper toasting the inside of a new oak barrel. (Bodegas Muga, Haro, Spain.)*

ABOVE *Racks of American oak barrels at Beaulieu Vineyards, Napa Valley, California.*

MAKING FORTIFIED WINES

As yeasts cannot work above 16 percent alcohol, wine above this level must have been fortified. Often this is done by adding brandy, as in Port or Sherry, or by adding neutral grape spirit as in the *Vin Doux Naturel* of Languedoc-Roussillon.

Originally wines were fortified in order to make them travel better: wines low in alcohol could easily spoil on long sea journeys. Or it made them taste better: when the British boycotted French wines during the wars of the seventeenth century, British merchants added brandy to the rough, astringent red wines of Portugal's Douro and created Port.

The term fortified covers a range of methods. *Sherries* are fortified after the alcoholic fermentation has finished. Brandy at 77 percent is added to *port* when the alcohol level in the fermenting wine reaches about 8 percent, killing the yeasts and producing a sweet wine. The process for *vin doux naturel* is similar to port but high strength, neutral spirit is used instead. *Madeira* uses a mixture of these methods depending upon the style wanted.

SOME OTHER TECHNIQUES

SKIN CONTACT

This technique is used for some white wines. The grapes are left to macerate in the juice for between four and 24 hours before being pressed. Skin contact extracts more aroma and flavor from the grapes. At times these flavors can be heavy and subtle and the wines age less well. Sometimes only a proportion of a wine has had skin contact.

BARREL FERMENTATION AND AGING

The use of new oak barrels, usually holding 225 liters (about 60 gallons) to give complexity to wine is increasing. The oak imparts vanilla as well as toasty flavors if the inside of the barrel has been given a high toasting. With prolonged use, the barrels lose their vanilla flavor. Also, because wood is slightly porous, there is a slow exchange between the air outside and the wine inside, which makes the wine rounder and smoother. New wood aging has to be used carefully, otherwise the wine is overwhelmed by the wood.

There are cheaper ways of adding oak flavor. Working on the same principle as the tea bag, oak chips tied up in a bag can be suspended in a vat.

3
THE WORLD'S VINEYARDS:

CALIFORNIA TO ARGENTINA BY WAY OF NEW ZEALAND

The abbreviations appearing on the charts indicate wine color:
R = Red; W = White; Ro = Rosé; Sp = Sparkling.
The abbreviations are ordered by size of production,
e.g. if R appears before W, then more red than white is produced.
The symbols indicating price are:
* Inexpensive, ** Medium priced, *** High price,
**** Among the world's most expensive bottles

CALIFORNIA AND U.S.

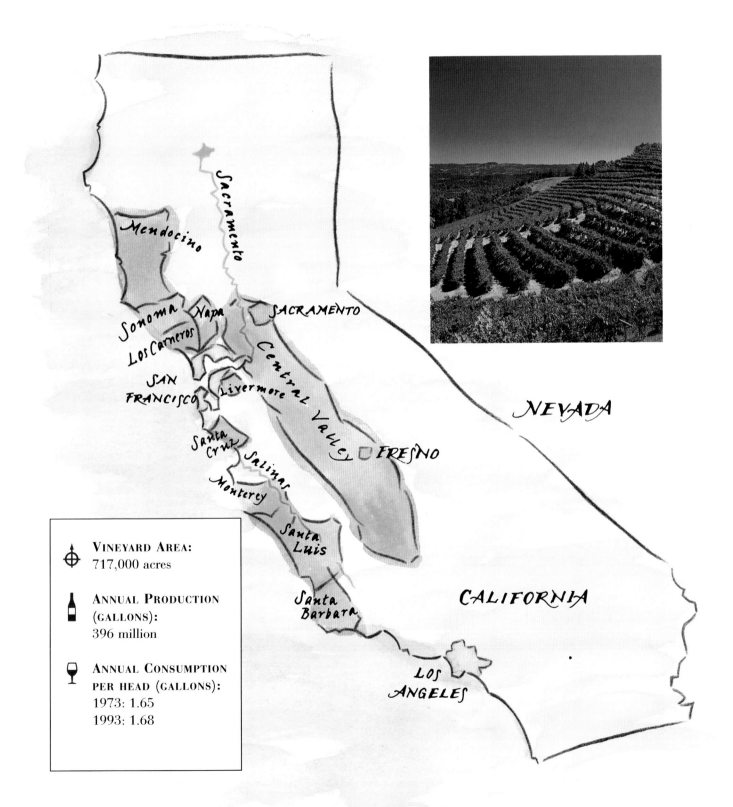

Sacramento

Mendocino

Sonoma Napa

Los Carneros

SACRAMENTO

SAN FRANCISCO

Livermore

Central Valley

FRESNO

NEVADA

Santa Cruz

Salinas

Monterey

Santa Luis

Santa Barbara

CALIFORNIA

LOS ANGELES

⊕ **VINEYARD AREA:**
717,000 acres

🍾 **ANNUAL PRODUCTION (GALLONS):**
396 million

🍷 **ANNUAL CONSUMPTION PER HEAD (GALLONS):**
1973: 1.65
1993: 1.68

ABOVE *The cold Californian coast, here at Point Reyes, which has such a moderating influence on the climate in California's premium vineyards.*

BELOW *Beringer Vineyards: the Rhine House built in 1883 by Jacob Beringer.*

I n 1976 Californian wines stunned the wine world by beating France's top wines, including Haut Brion and Mouton-Rothschild, at a blind tasting held in Paris. This shock result put California's wines onto the international scene: boosting their reputation at home and establishing one in Britain and elsewhere.

California's wine producing tradition dates back to the 1850s, but it has had a mixed history. There was rapid expansion in the second half of the nineteenth century, only to be halted by the arrival of phylloxera at the century's end. Natural devastation was followed by a man-made disaster: Prohibition, which lasted from 1920 until 1933. It wasn't until the 1960's that California got back onto the quality wine trail with the redevelopment of the Napa Valley and the building of wineries, epitomized by Mondavi's in Oakland. Unfortunately, many of the vineyards planted during the 1960's and 1970's were on rootstock that is not properly resistant to phylloxera. Phylloxera resurfaced in the late 1980's in California, and millions of dollars have been spent in replacing dead vines.

The silver lining in this disaster is that growers have the chance to rethink which are the best varieties to plant. The years 1990 to 1995 have seen the choice of wines coming out of California widening away from just the inevitable Chardonnay and Cabernet Sauvignon. However, although it is true that there is a growing interest among some winemakers and drinkers in varieties like Syrah and Sangiovese as well as a revaluing of California's native grape, Zinfandel, this has to be kept in perspective.

ABOVE *Mondavi's Oakville winery is a defining Napa landmark. It was opened in 1966.*

RIGHT *The vineyards of Carneros stretching down to the San Pablo Bay.*

Colombard remains easily the most widely planted variety (51,174 acres). Most of this is grown in the hot Central Valley and used to make jug wine. So, too, are most of the 27,180 acres of Chenin Blanc. Zinfandel (34,282 acres) is the second most popular variety; again much planted in the Central Valley. Of the premium international varieties Chardonnay (34,282 acres) and Cabernet Sauvignon (28,088 acres) dominate quality wine production. Even the currently "hot" varietal Merlot has only 3,877 acres planted while there is less then 120 acres of apparently fashionable Syrah in the entire state of California.

CALIFORNIA
NORTH OF THE BAY

AREA	MENDOCINO	SONOMA COUNTY	NAPA VALLEY	CARNEROS
Climate	Cool by coast, markedly hotter inland.	Cool by Sonoma, warmer by Santa Rosa.	Cooler in south by Napa, much hotter by Calistoga.	One of the coolest areas because of the St. Pablo Bay fogs.
Chief grapes	Chardonnay, Cabernet Sauvignon, Merlot, Zinfandel	Cabertnet Sauvignon, Chardonnay	Chardonnay, Cabernet Sauvignon, Merlot, Pinot Noir, Sauvignon Blanc, Zinfandel	Chardonnay, Pinot Noir
Size (acres)	11,295	27,500	28,716	5,305
Avg. Vol. (gal.)	n/a	n/a	n/a	n/a
Soils	Clay and gravel	Sandstone and shale	Gravel, sand and volcanic	Thin topsoil with clay underneath
Style	Toward the coast well adapted to sparkling wine production. Inland rich Cabs and Zins.	Well adapted to Chardonnay of varying richness. Often quite leafy Cabernets.	Powerful blackcurrant Cabernet Sauvignon, though tannins can be too much.	The cooler climate gives crisper, more vivid fruit and elegant wines.
Quality/buying tips	Quality runs from reliable to very good.	Wide range of quality. Sonoma produces some of the state's best Chardonnay.	A range of styles but some of California's best Cabernet Sauvignon comes from here.	Some of California's best Pinot Noir and Chardonnay.
Price	**—***	**—***	**—****	**—***
Best producers	Fetzer, Frey, Guenoc, Konocti, Lazy Creek, Roederer Estate, Scharffenberger	Buena Vista, Clos du Bois, DeLoach, Duxoup, Gallo, Iron Horse, Laurel Glen, Sonoma Cutrer	Beringer, BV, Caymus, Clos du Val, Frogs Leap, Mondavi, Newton, Opus One, Stags Leap, Stony Hill, ZD Pepperwood Grove	Acacia, Domaine Carneros, Carneros Creek, Rasmussen, Saintsbury
Best vintages	W: 94, 91, 90, 87, 85 R: 94, 92, 91, 90, 88, 87	W: 94, 93, 91, 90, 88 R: 93, 91, 90, 85, 84, 83	W: 94, 93, 91, 90, 88 R: 94, 93, 91, 90, 85, 84, 83	W: 94, 93, 91, 90, 88 R: 94, 93, 91, 90, 85, 84, 83

ABOVE *The spectacularly-sited vineyards of Mount Eden in the Santa Cruz Mountains.*

Parts of California have an ideal range of climates for growing quality wine grapes. The crucial factor is always distance from the Pacific Ocean and whether its fogs can penetrate inland. The persistent fogs are caused by the cold California Current from the Arctic that flows down along the Californian coast. The meeting of cold water and hot air over the land mass creates daily fogs from May through to September. These fogs lower the temperature significantly around the coast and they get drawn inland either up river valleys or through gaps in the coastal mountain range.

The surprising effect is that there are some decidedly cool climate growing areas at a latitude where one might expect all grapes to be roasted by the sun. The changes in the thirty miles from Carneros to Calistoga is a good example of this climatic change.

The vineyards on the low hills of Carneros are cooled by the mists and wind coming off the San Pablo Bay. This means that although Carneros is on the same latitude as Athens its actual climate is cool enough both to produce finely flavored Chardonnay and Pinot Noir and to retain good levels of acidity in the grapes. Paradoxically as you travel northward up the Napa Valley, the summer temperatures go up, as the cooling effects decline. By Rutherford, 17 miles up the Napa Valley from Carneros, the temperatures are ideal for growing Cabernet Sauvignon and Merlot. Then by Calistoga, at the top of the valley and only 12 miles on from Rutherford, it is hot enough to grow Grenache and Zinfandel. Climatic variations like this can be found throughout California.

There are some very fine Californian wines now being made: Cabernet Sauvignons, whose fruit and tannins are in balance; Chardonnays, which have delicacy as well as power; complex Pinot Noirs, especially from cooler areas like Carneros; and increasingly fine Zinfandels, which have real character rather than just raw brute fruit.

Unfortunately there is still a tendency for many winemakers to overdo the oak as well as producing overalcoholic wines. There are too many white wines, particularly Chardonnays, at 14 percent alcohol which just leave the drinker stunned after a couple of glasses. Too many "Chardonnays" whose fruit is hidden under a wooden layer of vanilla, making some of them quite undrinkable. There have also been some monster Cabernets whose level of tannin has been so high that it is doubtful whether it will ever soften before the fruit dies away.

There are a number of American and foreign firms making very drinkable bottle fermented sparkling wines in California. These firms have searched out the cooler growing areas, especially in western Sonoma and the cooler parts of Mendocino County. Foreign companies include Roederer in Mendocino, Moët Chandon and Mumm in Napa, and Taittinger at Domaine Carneros. Also in Carneros are the two leading Spanish Cava companies: Codorniu and Freixenet. Among the leading native U.S. companies are Schramsberg and Iron Horse, the latter making some of the best sparkling wine in California.

CALIFORNIA
SOUTH AND EAST OF THE BAY

AREA	LIVERMORE	SANTA CRUZ MTS.	MONTEREY
Climate	Low rainfall: winter and spring, hot summers but cool nights.	Relatively cool with considerable variations within the mountains.	Cool by Pacific Ocean but hot and dry inland.
Size (acres)	1,156	203	2,247
Avg. Vol. (gal.)	n/a	n/a	n/a
Soils	Gravel	Shale	Silt and Loam
Chief grapes	Cabernet Sauvignon, Chardonnay, Sauvignon Blanc, Sémillon	Chardonnay, Cabernet Sauvignon, Pinot Noir	Chardonnay, Chenin Blanc, Riesling, Cabernet Sauvignon, Pinot Noir, Zinfandel
Style	Rich, full-flavored wines – often tropical fruit style. Chardonnay dominates.	Range of styles but often rich buttery Chardonnays and deep-colored reds.	Chardonnay dominates.
Quality/buying tips	Look out for Sauvignons and Sémillon. Reds are pleasant but rarely exciting.	Individual wines – well worth seeking out.	Variable: from cheap jug wines to a few high quality ones at top end.
Aging potential	3–6	3–10	Most drink young, best up to 7
Price	*–**	**–***	*–***
Best producers	Fenestra, J. Lohr, Wente	David Bruce, Bonny Doon, Mount Eden, Page Mill, Ridge	Chalone, Estancia Monterey Estate, Jekel, Smith & Hook, Ventana
Best vintages	94, 93, 90	94, 93, 90	94, 93

Excepting the furnace summer of heat of the Central Valley, there are also cool climate areas in this region.

SAN LUIS OBISPO	SANTA BARBARA	CENTRAL VALLEY	SIERRA FOOTHILLS
Warm and fairly low rainfall except for York Mountain which is much wetter and cooler.	Relatively cool due to Pacific Ocean's influence.	Hot and arid.	Depends upon height: varies between hot in Amador to markedly cooler and wetter in North Yuba.
6,355	7,428	194,003	1,848
n/a	n/a	n/a	n/a
Varied: limestone, shale and alluvial soils	Marine sandstone and shale	Clay and alluvial soils	Volcanic
Chardonnay, Sauvignon Blanc, Cabernet Sauvignon, Zinfandel	Chardonnay, Riesling, Cabernet Sauvignon and Pinot Noir	Chardonnay, Colombard, Chenin Blanc, Zinfandel	Sauvignon Blanc, Zinfandel
Chardonnay varies from tart to fat. Soft easy Cabernet, power. Soft easy Cabernet, powerful spicy Zins.	Rich Chardonnays and some wonderfully fruity Pinot Noirs.	Mainly cheap jug wine. High yields often giving bland wine.	Zinfandel dominates: powerful wines – occasionally over-ripe. Crisp Sauvignon.
Interesting area especially for reds.	Top producers are among California's best.	Most are inexpensive.	The best are interesting and worth exploring.
2–6	5–10	Drink young	Up to 5
–*	**–***	*	**
Clairborne & Churchill, Maison Deutz, Edna Valley Winery, Meridian, Wild Horse	Au Bon Climat, Byron, Qupé, Vita Nova	Château de Leu, Mondavi Woodbridge	Amador Foothill Winery, Black Sheep Vintners, Boeger, Noceto, Renaissance, Shenandoah
94, 93, 90	94, 91	94	94, 93, 90

ABOVE *Domaine Carneros: Taitinger's imposing, if somewhat incongruous, sparkling wine outpost in California.*

The Californian wine industry is an interesting mix of big corporations, such as Nestlé (which owns Beringer in Napa and Meridian Vineyards in the Central Coast area), Seagram with Sterling (Napa Valley), and Mondavi; and many enterprising and determined individualists. In Gallo, California has the largest wine company in the world. But alongside these big corporations, there are laid-back individuals like Andy and Debbie Cutter of Duxoup, who give all of their oak barrels a name and are determined not to produce more than 2,000 cases a year, so that they can continue to go to the opera and hang onto their laid-back lifestyle.

One of the most interesting Californian characters is Randall Grahm. At Bonny Doon in the Santa Cruz Mountains, Grahm has led the reaction against wall-to-wall Chardonnay and Cabernet Sauvignon. He has produced a series of blends using Mediterranean grape varieties such as Syrah, Grenache, and Mourvèdre for the reds and whites from Marsanne and Roussanne. Grahm is also interested in Italian varieties as well as Riesling and Chenin Blanc. Given California's range of climates it seems entirely sensible to want to explore as wide a spectrum of grape varieties and their different tastes as possible.

Grahm is sometimes viewed as an eccentric aging hippy. This is to underestimate an articulate and thoughtful observer of the wine scene. Grahm is shrewd enough to realize that today's wine enthusiasts are

ABOVE *Iron Horse in Western Sonoma which makes one of the best of the Californian sparklers.*

RIGHT *Duxoup: only a few miles away from Gallo, but its absolute antithesis—small scale, idiosyncratic and very personal—all the barrels have their own names!*

ABOVE *Gallo's premium vineyard in Dry Creek Valley, Sonoma with large modern winery in background.*

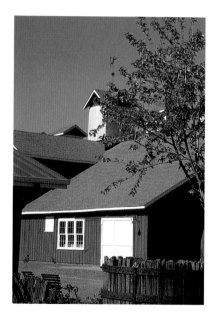

ABOVE *New Frog's Leap winery at Rutherford, Napa.*

RIGHT *Newton's sculptured vineyards on the western edge of the Napa Valley.*

looking for interesting and unusual bottles of wine and that there is a market for flavors that are different from buttery Chardonnay and black-curranty Cabernet Sauvignon.

There are also individuals who have had the opportunity to create remarkably beautiful vineyards. One such is Peter Newton. Newton is an Englishman, who having sold Sterling to Coca-Cola in 1977 (subsequently sold to Seagram), created a spectacular new vineyard on the steep hillsides above St. Helena, overlooking the Napa Valley. In spring the vineyard is particularly beautiful with the fresh green vine shoots, wild flowers, and the ornamental gardens that Newton and his wife, Su Hua, created to hide the winery. The Newton Merlot is particularly good.

As in other vine-growing countries, there is increasing interest in organic viticulture and in sustainable agriculture. This is true both of smaller wineries such as John and Julie William's Frog's Leap and large corporations such as Fetzer in Mendocino County, now owned by the distillers Brown Forman, and by Gallo in its premium vineyards in Sonoma. Given their often dry climate, Californian vine growers ought to be well placed to use organic methods. It is always easier and safer to eschew the chemical armory when rot and disease is less of a problem than it is in humid climates such as southern England and parts of New Zealand.

California is the only U.S. state to have a real wine culture. Having a strong home market and a significant proportion of the local population that is interested in wine has doubtless helped encourage Californian winemakers. Wine tourism has become very important, and the Napa Valley is arguably the world's number one center.

The Texas wine industry is very recent. In 1975 there were less than 25 acres planted. Most of the wine is varietally labeled with Chenin Blanc as the leading grape followed by Sauvignon Blanc, Chardonnay and Cabernet Sauvignon. There is also a small amount of bottle fermented sparkling wine being made. Leading wineries include Cap Rock, Fall Creek, Llano Estacado, Pheasant Ridge, and Ste. Geniviere.

VINEYARD AREA:
2,965 acres

PRODUCTION:
Just below one million cases

RIGHT *Fall Creek vineyards on the north-west shores of Lake Buchanan.*

OREGON AND WASHINGTON

OREGON

Although there are many fewer vines in Oregon than neighboring Washington, Oregon has had much more of the spotlight. Pinot Noir, the grape variety that challenges and tantalizes, is the reason. Success in the late 1970's and early 1980's made it seem that Oregon was the place for Pinot Noir. Wines from David Lett's Eyrie Vineyards and Dick Erath's Knudsen Erath were acclaimed. In 1988 Robert Drouhin, one of the leading Burgundian merchants, planted Pinot Noir here and built a winery. Oregon's name became linked with Pinot Noir.

However, the climate is very variable and vintages inconsistent. Doubts have crept in: Oregon Pinot Noirs are good but are they that good?

VINEYARD AREA:
Oregon: 4,900 acres
Washington: 33,850 acres

ANNUAL PRODUCTION:
Oregon: n/a
Washington: 3 million
cases

BEST RECENT VINTAGES:
92, 91, 90, 89

Most of the vineyards are in the Williamette Valley with many of the best-known producers just to the south or west of Portland in the volcanic red earth of the Dundee Hills. Oregon's climate is quite cool and wet: much closer to that of Burgundy than California. Most of the rain falls during the winter and spring but a cool summer brings the problem of autumn rains arriving before the grapes are fully ripe. Of course, Pinot Noir is very susceptible to rot!

Chardonnay, Riesling, and Pinot Gris are grown as well as Pinot Noir. Because of the variations from vintage to vintage, Oregon Chardonnay, even from the same property, ranges from lean and lemony to rich and buttery. There is also a small amount of Cabernet Sauvignon but it is difficult to get this late ripener properly mature.

Pinot Gris has become a fashionable variety and some of Oregon's best bottles are made from this variety. Growers in California are beginning to pick up on this Pinot, too.

Other leading producers include Amity, Argyle, where Rollin Soles makes very good bottle fermented sparkling wines under the guidance of Australia's Brian Croser, Elk Cove (good Pinot Noir), King Estate Ponzi, especially for Pinot Gris and Riesling, and Rex Hill for Pinot Gris again.

Farther south from the Williamette, vines are grown in the warmer Rogue and Umpqua Valleys. The leading varieties in Rogue are Cabernet Sauvignon and Chardonnay, while Pinot Noir, Chardonnay, and Riesling take the lead in Umpqua.

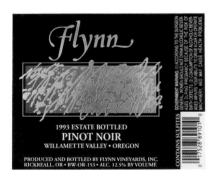

RIGHT *Picking Pinot Noir at Sokol Blosser winery in the Williamette Valley, Oregon. Mount Hood is 65 miles beyond.*

WASHINGTON

Despite its infancy—the modern Washington wine industry dates from 1962—this state is the largest producer of premium grapes in the United States after California.

The vine-growing conditions are very different from those in Oregon. Most of the vineyards are planted in semidesert conditions to the east of the Casade Mountains. Here, over 200 miles from the Pacific, the climate is continental. Summers are hot, winters cold, and there is little rain. Only irrigation allows the vine to survive here and precautions have to be taken against the severe winter cold, otherwise the vines are killed by the low temperatures.

Columbia Valley is the most important area with some 6,285 acres, followed by the Yakima Valley with a little over 4,200 acres. The main white varieties are Chardonnay, Riesling, Sauvignon Blanc, and Sémillon. For the reds, it is Cabernet Sauvignon and Merlot with a small amount of not very successful Pinot Noir. Washington whites have crisp, crunchy fruit. The reds have an intensity of berry fruit which comes from slow ripening.

Leading producers include Arbor Crest (Chardonnay and Merlot), Columbia, Covey Run, Hedges, Hogue Cellars (Cabernet Franc, Merlot, and Sémillon), Quilceda Creek, and Woodward Canyon (Chardonnay and Cabernet/Merlot blends). Château Ste. Michelle in Seattle is the largest producer with a big range of wines, including late harvest and sparkling. Kiona, in the Yakima Valley, produces very good value late harvest Gewürztraminer and Riesling, along with a fine barrel fermented Chardonnay.

The future looks exciting for Washington wine.

ABOVE *Good value—Kiona Late Harvest Riesling.*

RIGHT *Picking Pinot Noir for Rex Hill at Dundee Hills vineyards, Oregon.*

RIGHT *Machine harvesting of Gewürztraminer at Covey Run Vintners, Yakima Valley, Washington.*

 VINEYARD AREA:
29,040 acres

 ANNUAL PRODUCTION:
figures not available

EASTERN UNITED STATES

After many years of mainly using native American vines (*vitis labrusca*) which give wine a marked foxy taste, interesting things are happening with the number of producers using noble varieties (*vitis vinifera*) expanding rapidly in traditional areas like New York State and in new quality wine-producing states like Virginia.

New York State is the second largest grape growing area in the United States with some 29,040 acres of vines. The passing of the 1976 Farm Winery Act caused an explosion of new plantings and there are now about a hundred wineries producing just over 264,000 gallons of wine a year. There are four vine growing areas: Lake Erie, the Finger Lakes, the Hudson Valley, and Long Island, which is the most exciting with its maritime climate. Long Island now has 18 wineries with 1,300 acres of vines planted.

Although hybrid vines such as Seyval Blanc and Vidal for whites, and Baco Noir and Maréchal Foch for reds, plus Concord (a native American variety), remain important in New York, it is the greatly increased plantings of premium varieties which has created the interest. Chardonnay, Gewürztraminer, Pinot Blanc, Riesling, and Sauvignon Blanc are the white varieties planted with Cabernet Franc, Cabernet Sauvignon, Merlot, and Pinot Noir for the reds. With the exception of Pinot Noir, the reds are most successful on Long Island. Leading producers include Canandaigua, Glenora, Knapp, Lamoreaux Landing, Wagner Vineyards (Finger Lakes), Clinton Vineyards, Millbrook (Hudson Valley), Bedell, Bridgehampton, Hargrave Vineyard, Lenz, Palmer, and Pindar Vineyards (Long Island).

Although vines were first planted in Virginia early in the seventeenth century and Thomas Jefferson had an estate at Monticello, the revival of winemaking here is recent. So far, Chardonnay has been the most successful variety but there are also promising reds from Cabernet Sauvignon and Merlot. There are now nearly fifty wineries and leading producers include Barboursville, Horton, Tarara, and Williamsburg.

CANADA

VINEYARD AREA:
23,635 acres

ANNUAL PRODUCTION:
5.5 million cases

ANNUAL CONSUMPTION PER HEAD (GALLONS):
1973: 1.4
1993: 2.16

Ice-wine is Canada's best claim to international fame. Once a specialty largely confined to parts of Germany and Austria, where it is called *eiswein*, it is now made regularly in Ontario, around the lakes of Erie and Ontario, and in British Columbia.

Although some vineyards were established in the nineteenth century, the modern Canadian wine industry is very young, just like that of Washington. The 1980's were the real starting point. The two most important areas are Ontario and British Colombia. A small amount of wine is also made in Quebec and Nova Scotia. Everywhere else in Canada the winters are too harsh and the growing season too short for vines to be grown successfully.

Quebec averages 250,000 bottles a year but spring frost can reduce this drastically. The best-known producers are Les Arpents de Neige and Vignoble de l'Orpailleur. One of the partners in l'Orpailleur is Hervé Durand, who has a vineyard in the Midi where he is experimenting with making wine by using the methods of the Ancient Romans. Nova Scotia has 145 acres of vines.

ONTARIO

VINEYARD AREA:
14,800 acres

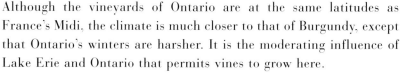
ANNUAL PRODUCTION:
3.3 million cases

Although the vineyards of Ontario are at the same latitudes as France's Midi, the climate is much closer to that of Burgundy, except that Ontario's winters are harsher. It is the moderating influence of Lake Erie and Ontario that permits vines to grow here.

One particularity of Ontario wine is the use of hybrids such as Baco Noir, Maréchal Foch, Seyval Blanc, and Vidal. These varieties are chosen because they are well adapted to the rigors of Canada's climate. Vidal has been particularly successful; some of the best ice wines are made from it. Chardonnay, Gewürztraminer, and Riesling are the leading "noble" white varieties. Apart from the sweet wines, Chardonnay has been the most successful. The reds are made from Cabernet Franc, Cabernet Sauvignon, Gamay, Merlot, and Pinot Noir.

Best producers include: Château des Charmes, Henry of Pelham, Inniskillin (ice-wine in particular) and Vineland Estates.

ABOVE *Harvest time at Lang Vineyards, Okanagan Valley.*

BRITISH COLUMBIA

The British Columbia vineyards are much farther north than those of Ontario. They are on the same latitude as Reims in northern France.

It was the decision to grub out the hybrids that created the modern British Columbia wine industry. The vineyards are centered in the Okanagan Valley, which is an arid desert, having less than 6 inches of rain annually. Although summer temperatures are very high here, there is a big daily variation because of the cool nights and this is an important factor in developing flavor.

Riesling is widely planted along with Auxerrois, Chardonnay, Pinot Blanc and Gewürztraminer. Pinot Noir and Merlot are planted for the reds.

Best producers include Blue Mountain Vineyard and Cellars, Gray Monk, Mission Hill, Quail's Gate, and Sumac Ridge.

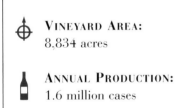

VINEYARD AREA:
8,834 acres

ANNUAL PRODUCTION:
1.6 million cases

PORTUGAL

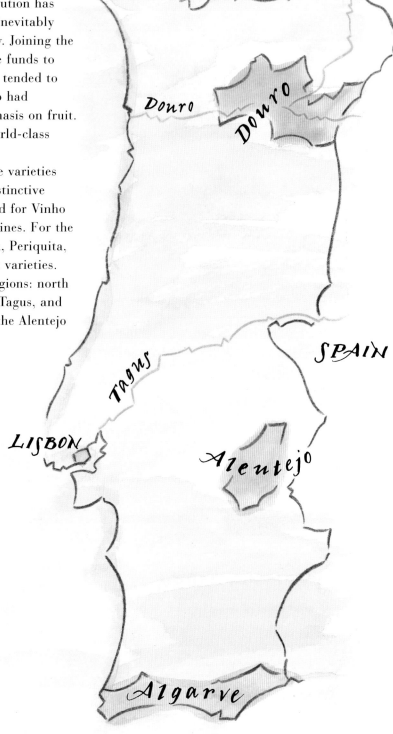

A s in Spain, the modern wine revolution has arrived in neighboring Portugal. Inevitably progress is patchy but change is underway. Joining the European Union has helped to provide the funds to modernize. Traditional tannic reds, which tended to dry out long before their fierce tannic grip had lessened, are giving way to a greater emphasis on fruit. In Port and Madeira, Portugal has two world-class famous fortified wines.

There are a number of indigenous grape varieties which give Portuguese wines their own distinctive character. Alvarinho and Loureiro are used for Vinho Verdes, and Arinto de Bucelas for white wines. For the reds there are Baga, especially in Bairrada, Periquita, and Touriga Nacional, the best of the port varieties.

The country divides into three broad regions: north of the Douro, between the Douro and the Tagus, and then the southern part with the plains of the Alentejo and the coastal Algarve.

 VINEYARD AREA:
988,400 acres

 ANNUAL PRODUCTION:
2.11 million gallons

 ANNUAL CONSUMPTION PER HEAD (GALLONS):
1973: 21.2
1993: 12.4

PORTUGAL
WINE REGIONS AND PRODUCERS

REGION	WINE/AREA	STYLE	RECOMMENDED PRODUCERS
North of Douro	Vinho Verde (W)	Light spritz whites	Quinta da Aveleda, Palácio de Brejoeira, Solar das Bouças
	Duoro (R, W, Ro)	Soft full bodied reds, aromatic whites	Ferreira (Barca Velha), Quinta Do Cotto
Douro – Tagus (Lisbon)	Dão (R, W)	Often harsh, tannic reds, lacking fruit. Some improvements on the way	Caves Alianca, Caves Sáo Joáo, Duque de Viseu, Fonseca Successores, Sogrape, Quinta de Saes
	Bairrada (R, W, Ro)	Very good reds and fast improving whites	Caves Alianca, Caves Sáo Joáo, Luis Pato, Sogrape
	Bucelas (W)	High acidity, needs age to soften	Quinta da Romeira, Caves Velhas, Prova Régia
South of Lisbon	Setubal	Fortified Muscat, the 20-year-old can be very fine. Plus some reds.	Muscat Fonseca Successores, JP Vinhos; Reds: Quinta da Bacalhôa
	Alentejo	Fast improving area especially for reds	Fonseca Successores, Herdade de Cartuxa, Quinta do Carmo, JP Vinhos

ABOVE *High training of vines in Madeira.*

PORT

This fortified wine is made from grapes grown on the dry, steep sided slopes of the Douro Valley. The wine ferments until it has reached around 7% alcohol, when *aguardente*, a colorless grape spirit is added and the fermentation is stopped. Roughly one part of *aguardente* is added to four parts of wine. Because about half the grape sugar still remained when the spirit was added, port is always sweet. Most port is then matured in "lodges" (warehouses) in Vila Nova de Gaia, a suburb of Oporto on the Atlantic coast.

MADEIRA

Some of the longest-lived fortified wines in the world, capable of living at least 150 years, come from the Atlantic island of Madeira. The following four main styles of Madeira are named after the grape variety used.

SERCIAL is the driest style made. Between a fino sherry and amontillado in weight, it makes a very good aperitif.

VERDELHO is demi-sec and is more rounded without the vibrancy of Sercial.

BUAL is medium sweet, often quite medicinal in flavor.

MALMSEY is the sweetest style, mellow and raisiny like a rich fruit cake.

Top-quality Madeira is rare and expensive.

BELOW *Ruby and tawny ports made from grapes grown on the slopes of the Douro Valley.*

PORT STYLES

Port divides into two broad styles: ruby and tawny. Port that is aged for a length of time in wood is called tawny because the wines gradually lose their color. Ruby styles are bottled relatively early.

STYLE	DEFINITION
RUBY TYPE	
Ruby	This is the cheapest style and should have three years aging.
Late Bottled Vintage (LBV)	From a single year and aged in wood for 4–6 years. It is often filtered before bottling, so decanting is not necessary.
Vintage character	Similar to an LBV but is a blend of several years.
Crusted	A blend of several vintages which is then matured. As the Port is unfiltered, it will throw a deposit (crust) and needs decanting.
Single Quinta	From a single estate (Quinta) customarily from a good vintage. Bottled after 2 years in cask.
Vintage	Port which is declared a vintage by a shipper during its second year in cask. It is then bottled. It is very rare to declare more than three vintages a decade. Vintage normally needs 10 years' minimum before it is ready to drink. The finest vintages often require much more
TAWNY STYLE	
Tawny port	Should be aged a minimum of five years in wood. Cheap tawnies can often be a raw blend of ruby and white port.
Aged tawnies	Aged in wood for a specified length of time—10, 20, 30, 40 years. Old tawnies can have a fine raisiny, figgy character.
Colheita tawnies	From a single vintage and matured in cask for a minimum of seven years. Can be the best of tawnies.
White port	Drunk as an aperitif. It is often quite dry but it is usually sweetened for export.

Recommended producers: A.A. Cálem, Churchill Graham, Cockburn's, Croft, Delaforce, Dow, Ferreira, Fonseca, Graham's Niepoort, Quinta do Noval, Sandeman, Taylor, Fladgate & Yeatman, Warre.

Best Vintage Port years: 45, 48, 55, 60, 63, 66, 70, 75, 77, 82, 83, 85, 91

ABOVE *Looking down on the little town of Pinhao in the heart of the Douro Valley, Portugal.*

ABOVE *Vintage bottles from the Madeira Wine Company.*

SPAIN

FRANCE

Galicia

PORTUGAL

Rioja   Navarre

Castilla de Leon

Aragon

BARCELONA

Catalonia   Penedés

MADRID

Tagus

Castilla
La Mancha

Valencia

Andalucia

Jerez

GIBRALTAR

⊕ **VINEYARD AREA:**
3.57 million acres (1989)

🍷 **ANNUAL PRODUCTION:**
798 million gallons

🍷 **ANNUAL CONSUMPTION
PER HEAD (GALLONS):**
1973: 17.1
1993: 8.3

MARQUES DE
MONISTROL
CASA FUNDADA EN 1882
GRAN TRADICION
11,5%Vol.   75 cl.
ELABORADO POR MARQUES DE MONISTROL, S.A.
MONISTROL D'ANOIA - SANT SADURNI D'ANOIA - ESPAÑA
R.E. 20-456/B   EMB. 1260/B
CAVA

MARQUÉS DE MURRIETA
ESTATE BOTTLED
YGAY   RIOJA
EMBOTELLADO EN ORIGEN
BODEGAS MARQUÉS DE MURRIETA, S.A.
LOGROÑO . ESPAÑA . SPAIN
RESERVA 1989

TORRES

FUNDADA 1870

Sangre de Toro

PRODUCIDO Y EMBOTELLADO POR
MIGUEL TORRES, S.A. - VILAFRANCA DEL PENEDÈS - PRODUCTO DE ESPAÑA

PENEDÈS
13% vol   Denominación de Origen   e 75 cl

BELOW *Vineyard landscape south of Cenicero, La Rioja, Spain.*

S pain is very much a land of wine. Many of the traditional images of Spain are linked to wine such as peasants drinking straight from a wine pouch or dark, besashed Spaniards skillfully pouring sherry in a thin golden stream and from a great height into glasses using the traditional venencia. Spain offers venerable bottles of Rioja, good value sparkling wines from Catalonia, the incredible range of flavors in Jerez, and, until recently, bottles of rough Spanish wines. In the past many a partygoer's hangover was instigated by an oversufficiency of Don Cortez, Carafino, and other cheap brands.

But the quality of wine from Spain has increased dramatically over the last seven or eight years. In the past the only areas consistently producing quality wine were Rioja and Jerez along with the Torres family in Penedès near Barcelona. Although some very poor wine is still made and sold in Spain, well made, often good-value, wines can now be found all over the country. Because of this exports of wine have boomed. Unfortunately in the mid-1990's, Spain, especially the southern part of the country, has been hit by a prolonged drought.

NORTHERN SPAIN

REGION	GALICIA	RIBERA DEL DUERO*	CASTILLE – LEÓN	RIOJA
DO	Rias Baixas Ribeiro	As above	Rueda Toro	As above
Soils	—	Limestone and chalk	—	Limestone/silt and clay
Climate	Relatively cool, high rainfall, maritime climate due to Atlantic Ocean.	Harsh winters, short hot summer but with cool nights.	As Ribera.	More Atlantic influence than in Castille with slightly cooler summer temperatures. SE Rioja more Mediterranean.
Grapes	Albariño, Palomino, Torrontés (W) Garnacha (R)	Tempranillo, Cabernet Sauvignon, Merlot, Malbec	Verdejo, Maccabeu, Palomino, Sauvignon Blanc (W) Garnacha, Tempranillo (R)	Cariñena, Graciano, Tempranillo (R) Maccabeu, Malvasia (W)
Size (acres)	14,826	22,807	40,770	116,137
Avg. Vol. (gal.)	8.39 million	3.96 million	5.07 million	43.76 million
Style/taste	Albariño – crisp, peachy, apricotty.	Mainly powerful, long lived reds.	W: now fresh, fruity, depth of flavor. R: chunky, full-bodied.	W: traditionally full-bodied and oaky. R: vary in style from relatively early drinking to long-lived. Vanilla oaky character.
Quality/buying tips	Albariño is easily best wine but expensive.	Variable quality but can be among Spain's best reds.	Rueda is making some of Spain's best whites. Toro's reds are good.	Some of Spain's best reds but standards are variable.
Aging potential	Drink young	5–50 years	R: 3–10	Res: GR:
Best producers	Adegas la Eiras, Lapetena, Lager de Cervera, Santiago Ruiz	Arroyo, Boada de Roa, Hacienda el Monasterio, Montevan-nos, Pedrosa. Pesquera, Vega Sicilia	Marqués de Griñon, Hermanos Lurton, Marqués de Riscal	Berberana, CUNE, Marqués de Murreita, Martinez Bujanda, Montecillo, Muga, Riojanas (Monte Real)
Price	*–***	**–****	**–***	**–***
Best vintages	Usually drink youngest	94, 91, 90, 87	94, 91, 90	94, 92, 91, 87, 85, 83, 82

*Abbreviations: Res: Reserva. GR: Gran Reserva. * Ribera del Duero: in Castille-León but with entry of its own. **Penedès is in Catalonia bu*

With the exception of Jerez, Spain's best wines come from the north of the country. This is largely because the climate is more temperate with the summers less scorchingly hot and dry.

NAVARRE	ARAGON	CATALONIA	PENEDÈS**
As above	Campo de Borja Somontano	Alella, Costers de Segre Priorato (P)	As above
Gravel over chalk	Varied	Varied includes granite, limestone, sand	Varied
Relatively wet and cool in north to hot and dry in south.	Dry and hot, except for cooler Pyrennean foothills.	Mediterranean.	Mediterranean.
Tempranillo, Cabernet Sauvignon	Granacha, Moristel, Tempranillo (R) Maccabeu, Moscatel (W)	Cabernet Sauvignon, Garnacha, Cariñena, Tempranillo (R); Parellada, Macabeo, Xarello, Chardonnay, Moscatel (W)	Garnacha, Cariñena, Tempranillo (R); Parellada, Macabeo, Xarello, Chardonnay (W)
44,230	108,700	120,510	63,580
14 million	21.13 million	21.14 million	45.15 million
Similar to Rioja but more emphasis on international grape varieties.	Very varied: light but flavorsome reds and whites from Somontano.	Best known for Cava – more earthy, fuller flavor than its rival: Champagne. Still wines from Raimat. Priorato is an amazingly powerful red.	Wide range of styles from fresh whites and reds to full bodied-wines of both colors which need to be aged.
Promising area – good value in the 3 colors.	Somontano is widely tipped for stardom.	At its best Cava offers good value bubbles.	Some of Spain's best reds and whites, especially from Torres.
3–15	Generally drink young	3–15	3–25+
Cenalsa, Chivite, Las Campanas, Magaña, Monte Ory, Ochoa, Senorío de Sarria	Borja Coop, COVISA, Bodegas San Somantano de Sobrarbe	Castellblanch, Codorníu, Freixenet, Juvé y Camps, Marqués de Monistrol, Raimat, Segura Viudas; P: Barril, De Muller, Scala-Dei	Jean Leon, Masía Bach, Jaume Serra, Torres
**	*–**	*–***	**–****
94, 93, 91, 87, 85	Drink young	R: 94, 93, 91, 87, 85, 83, 82, 79, 75, 70, 64 W: 94, 91, 88	R: 94, 93, 91, 87, 85, 83, 82, 79, 75, 70, 64 W: 94, 91, 88

own entry for still wines. Cava has been included under Catalonia column.

ABOVE *The remarkable architecture of Bodegas Tondonia in Haro, the heart of Spain's Rioja.*

ABOVE *Manzanilla is the lightest type of fino, with a salty tang.*

Although Spain has the largest area of vineyards in the world, it is only the third largest wine producer after Italy and France. This is because of the lack of water in many parts of Spain, which means that fewer grapes per acre are produced. The problem is most acute in southern Spain.

Despite improvements in the south, the majority of the best table wines still come from northern Spain.

WINES FROM JEREZ (SHERRY)

From tangy, bone dry finos to sweet, raisiny concentrated Pedro Ximenez, sherry has a remarkable range of flavors. Sadly this range is little known and sherry is decidedly undervalued. This is partly because there is too much poor-quality sherry around. Outside Spain, there is widespread ignorance about how to serve Jerez, in particular the more delicate fino styles. Fino needs to be treated like a dry white wine: served chilled and the bottle drunk up in a couple of days. Unfortunately, because it is a fortified wine, it is assumed to be indestructible. Bottles of half-consumed fino left for months in a warm cupboard are no more drinkable than a white or red wine would be.

Sherry is much more than an aperitif wine. Its different styles can match many different dishes. One of the best matches is fino with seafood—especially shellfish. But a dry amontillado can be drunk with roast chicken, a dry oloroso with a rich duck dish while powerful, rich sweet olorosos can be drunk with rich desserts.

The principal grape planted is the Palomino along with some Pedro Ximenez, for sweeter styles. The local chalky albariza soil absorbs and retains the winter rainfall, which is essential if the vines are to survive the fierce and unrelenting heat of southern Spain's summer. The three main towns for making and maturing sherry are Jerez de la Frontera, Puerto de Santa María, and Sanlúcar de Barrameda.

Sherry starts off by being vinified in the same manner as a white wine. All the sugar is fermented out leaving a bone dry wine. However, for aging, oxidation is encouraged. Butts are filled with wine but a gap is left at the top. Here a white yeast substance called *flor* develops, forming a protective layer between the wine and the air. *Flor* develops best in spring and autumn as the most favorable temperature range is 60–70°F. It also develops irregularly: heavily in some butts, lightly in others and, in some, not at all. Barrels that develop a thick layer of *flor* become manzanillas and finos, lighter growths to amontillados, and those with no growth become olorosos.

Once *flor* has developed or not, the wines are fortified. In the case of manzanillas, finos, and amontillados the fortification is slight. Olorosos are fortified to around 18%. A mixture of alcohol and mature wine is used. Sweeter styles are sweetened at a later stage. Jerez wines now have regained the sole right to the word, sherry.

SOUTHERN SPAIN

The fortified wines are still the best, especially Jerez, but big improvements are being made with red wines.

REGION	CASTILLA–LA MANCHA	VALENCIA	ANDALUCIA
DO	Almansa, La Mancha, Méntrida, Valdepeñas	Alicante, Jumilla (Jum), Valencia (Val), Yecla (Yec)	Condado de Huelva (Con), Jerez, Malaga (Mal), Montilla (Mon)
Climate	Very hot summer, cold winter, very little rain	Hot, dry Mediterranean climate	Very hot summer, what rain there is falls in winter
Grapes	Airén; Garnacha, Tempranillo	Bobal, Garnacha, Monastrell, Moscatel	Airén, Poscatel, Palomino, Pedro Ximenez
Size (acres)	1.73 million	309,420	181,620
Avg. Vol. (gal.)	475.5 million	63.4 million	83.2 million
Style/taste	Mainly white. Some new style fresh whites but still many are heavy, oxidized. Reds vary from thin to fruitily drinkable.	Mainly alcoholic reds and heavy whites but some fresher, lighter reds and whites appearing. Sweet Muscat.	Mostly fortified wines, although some Montillas and lighter sherries are not. Big range from: bone dry to raisiny sweet.
Quality/buying tips	An improving area with some good everyday wines.	Sweet Muscats are a bargain. Wines from Jumilla improving.	Montilla is good value but rarely more than moderate quality.
Aging potential	Generally drink young	Mainly drink young	Mostly sold when ready to drink
Best producers	Casa de la Vina, Los Llanos, Marqués de Grinon, Felix Soles, Vinicola de Castilla (Castillo de Alhambra)	Jum: Altos de Pio, Domino de Alba, Schenk, Taja, Umbria Novel; Val: Schenk, Vincente Grandia Pla; Yec: Castano	Con: Bollullos; Mal: Lopez Hermanos, Scholtz Hermanos; Mon: Alvear, Gracia Hermanos Sherry, see below
Price	*–**	*–**	*–***
Best vintages	n/a	n/a	n/a

ABOVE *Palamo Fino vines planted in the superb albariza soil (almost pure chalk) of Emilio Lustau's Montegillilo vineyard north of Jerez de la Frontera, Spain.*

SOLERA SYSTEM: A MATURATION PROCESS

Casks are left to mature in large warehouses (*Bodegas*) in wooden casks. Mature wine is taken from cask and is replenished by a young wine. Rather than the older wine being diluted by the young wine, the young wine takes on the characteristics of the older wine.

STYLES

MANZANILLA: A fino from Sanlúcar de Barrameda. The lightest type of fino and supposed to have a salty tang from being aged by the sea.

FINO: Develops beneath the *flor*. The lightest style of sherry.

AMONTILLADO: A little fuller than a fino, deeper in color. Strictly should be a fino that has been left in a cask until the *flor* has fallen to the bottom.

PALO CORTADO: Began as a fino became an Amontillado but developed in color and ended up like a rich oloroso. Dry.

OLOROSO: Doesn't develop *flor*, so fortified to 18% and left outside in sun to develop baked, burnt taste. Its alcohol content increases through evaporation and can reach 24%. Traditionally dry.

CREAM: Sweetened oloroso.

PALE CREAM: Sweetened fino.

Almacenista sherries are rare and have been matured by small, private merchants. They are well worth trying. Lustau has the best-known range.

RECOMMENDED SHERRY PRODUCERS AND THEIR BRANDS/WINES

NAME	BRANDS (WINES)
Tomás Abad	Fino
Barbadillo	Manzanilla Fina, Eva (manzanilla), Solear (manzanilla pasada), Principe (amontillado), PX
Bobadilla	Victoria (fino)
Diez-Merito	Don Zoilo range
Domecq	La Ina (fino), Sibarita (palo cortado), Río Viejo (dry oloroso), Venerable (PX)
Garvey	Tío Guillermo (amontillado), Ochavico (oloroso)
González Byass	Tio Pepe (fino), Elegante (fino), Amontillado del Duque Seco y Muy Viejo, Apóstoles (dry old oloroso), Matusalem (sweet old oloroso)
Hidalgo	La Gitana (manzanilla fina), Jerez Cortado
Lustau	Peninsula (palo cortado), Old East India, plus Almacenista range
Sandeman	Royal Ambrosante (palo cortado), Royal Corregidor, Imperial Corregidor (oloroso)
Valdespino	Deliciosa, Montana (manzanilla), Innocente (fino), Tio Diego (amontillado), Don Tómas (amontillado), Pedro Ximénez Solera Superior

RIGHT The range in color of sherries is caused by varying degrees of oxidation, Oloroso (left) being more oxidized than Amontillado (center), and Manzanilla (right) being the lightest and least oxidized.

ITALY

I taly more than France is the land of vines and wine. From spectacular terraces in Alpine valleys to the sunbaked landscape of Sicily, everywhere there are vines. Tying with France, it is the world's leading wine producer. Some years France produces more wine but most years it is Italy that is ahead.

Much of Italy's wine is produced with European Union subsidies and distillation in mind. But equally Italy makes some of the world's best and most exciting wines. Frequently they have a characteristic bitter-sweet quality and native Italian grape varieties, such as Dolcetto, Nebbiolo, and Sangiovese, are often used. So how to tell the good from the bad before pulling the cork?

There is a quality system. The Denominazione di Origine (DOC) category was launched in 1963 and now covers about 12 percent of Italian production with around 230 DOCs. More recently the superior DOCG category was introduced. Only eight wines have this status, among them Asti Spumante, Barolo, and Chianti.

The DOC system has been widely criticized because, it is said, there are too many DOCs, many of the DOCs do not deserve their status, and that the regulations inhibit innovation and often militate against quality. Certainly regulations have been too restrictive with the result that many of Italy's best (and most expensive) wines such as Sassicaia or Tignanello are labeled as *vino da tavolo*—the lowest wine category!

However, the Italians do not have the French passion for subdivision. In France a top area such as Barolo would have been subdivided into Barolo Villages, various *crus* etc. In the 25 miles of Burgundy's Côte d'Or, there are about 70 appellations alone! It is much simpler for the consumer to remember Barolo and then be able to concentrate on who are the good producers.

Although there are some bargains, good Italian wine tends to be expensive. Sometimes the price tag is justified but too often the quality of the wine and the price do not match. Too often a fancy designer bottle and artful label has made the wine 25 percent more expensive than it should be. For some producers expensive wine is part of Italian chic.

Italy has some of the most beautiful vineyards in the world. Two of the most famous are Chianti in the rolling Tuscan landscape and the steep ridges of Barolo in Piedmont. There are many other lesser-known wine areas, such as the Abruzzo, that are equally attractive.

ABOVE *Juicy, early ripening Dolcetto grapes (Piedmont).*

ABOVE *A typical vineyard scene in the rolling Tuscan landscape.*

SWITZERLAND

AUSTRIA

FRANCE

Valle
D'Aosta

Trentino
Alto Adige

Friuli-
Venezia-
Giulia

Lombardy

Veneto

VENICE

Piedmont

Liguria

Emilia-
Romagna

Tuscany

Marches

Umbria

Abruzzi

ROME

Lazio

Molise

SARDINIA

Campania

Puglia

Basilicata

Calabria

SICILY

ABOVE *Aldo Conterno's estate in Barolo. Conterno is one of the area's most respected producers.*

MASSETO

Cru Superiore di Merlot

1989

MARCHESE LODOVICO A.

Imbottigliato all'origine da
TENUTA DELL'ORNELLAIA
Bolgheri - Italia

ITALIA 750 ml   12.5% vol

⊕ **VINEYARD AREA:**
3.46 million acres
(688,420 acres DOC/
DOCG)

🍾 **ANNUAL PRODUCTION:**
1.58 billion gallons

🍷 **ANNUAL CONSUMPTION**
PER HEAD (GALLONS):
1973: 28.9
1993: 15.3

NORTHERN ITALY

REGION	VALLE D'AOSTA	PIEDMONT AND LIGURIA	LOMBARDY
Leading DOC and DOCGs	Valle d'Aosta	DOCG: Asti, Barolo (Brl), Barbaresco (Bar), Gattinara DO: Barbera d'Alba, Barbera d'Asti, Dolcetto d'Alba, Dolcetto d'Asti, Dolcetto d'Dogliani, Roero (Ro)	Franciacorta, Lugana, Oltrepo Pavese, Valtellina
Climate	Cool Alpine	Still influenced by the Alps with moderate summers.	Hot on Po Valley Plain, cooler in foothills of Alps.
Size (acres)	235	92,662	44,478
Avg. Vol. (gal.)	87,602	33.79 million	16.27 million
Chief grape varieties	Moscato, Pinot Grigio (W) Barbera, Nebbiolo, Petit Rouge, Vien de Nus (R)	Barbera, Dolcetto, Nebbiolo (R) Arneis, Muscat (W)	Chardonnay, Pinot Blanc, Trebbiano, Tocai (W) Barbera, Bonarda, Cabernet Franc, Merlot, Nebbiolo (R)
Style	Light reds and crisp whites.	Wide range of styles: long-lived reds from Barolo and Barbaresco. Light sparkling Muscats as in Asti Spumante, Moscato di Asti. Juicy reds from Dolcetto; vibrantly fruity, acidic reds from Barbera.	Wide range of red and white plus sparkling wines in Franciacorta.
Quality/buying tips	Small production, mostly drunk locally.	Area producing some of Italy's greatest wines, esp. Barolo and Barbaresco. Increasingly good whites from Roero.	Large quantities of everyday drinking wine. Best areas Oltrepo Pavese and Valtellina for red and Lugana for white.
Aging potential	Most wines to be drunk young.	Barolo and Barbaresco: up to 30+; Barbera 3–7	Drink young.
Price	**	*–****	*–**
Best producers	Co-op Morgex et de la Salle, Ezio Voyat	Brl: Ascheri, A. Conterno, G. Conterno, Mascarello, Prunotto, Ratti, Scavino, Vietti, Voerzio; Bar: Ceretto, Gaja, Giacosa, Produttori del Barbaresco, Pio Cesare; Ro: Deltetto, Malvira, Rabino	Ca'del Boscom, Doria, Nino Negri, Mairano, Visconti, Zenato
Best vintages	93, 92, 91, 90, 89, 88	93, 91, 89, 88, 85, 82, 78, 74, 71, 70, 61, 47	n/a

TRENTINO/ALTO-ADIGE	VENETO	FRIULI-VENEZIA GIULIA	EMILIA-ROMAGNA
As above plus Teroldego Rotaliano	Bardolino, Soave and Recioto di Soave (So), Valpolicella and Reciotto de Valpolicella (Val)	Colli Orientali del Friuli, Collio, Friuli Grave	Albana di Romagna and Sangiovese di Romagna, Colli Piacentini, Lambrusco
Sub-Alpine for Alto-Adige: cold winters, hot summers.	Hot on plains around Venice, cooler farther north.	Similar to Veneto.	Hot dry summers, damp, foggy winters.
28,420	88,960	33,110	67,040
18.75 million	48.77 million	16.03 million	24.98 million
AA: Cabernet Sauvignon, Lagrein, Schiava (R) Chardonnay, Pinot Blanc, Pinot Grigio, Riesling (W) T: Pinot Blanc, Pinot Grigio, Moscato, Müller Thurgau (W); Marzemino, Schiava, Teroldego (R)	Chardonnay, Garganega, Pinot Blanc, Pinot Grigio, Trebbiano (W); Barbera, Cabernet Franc, Cabernet Sauvignon, Corvina Veronese, Merlot, Molinara, Pinot Noir, Rondinella (R)	Pinot Blanc, Pinot Gris Sauvignon, Tocai, Malvasia, Verduzzo	Albana, Chardonnay, Malvasia, Ortugo, Pinot Grigio, Sauvignon Blanc, Trebbiano (W) Barbera, Cabernet Sauvignon, Merlot, Lambrusco, Sangiovese (R)
AA: Vibrant, depth of fruit in both red and white T: Often dilute, uninteresting wines – grape yields are too high.	Very wide range – best reds have power and character while the best whites have crisp weight.	Crisp dry, tangy whites; perfumed reds.	Big range but fizzy Lambrusco is best known.
Some very good wine-makers in AA. Much more patchy in Trentino but it does have good sparkling wines.	Bitter-sweet, powerful Amarone della Valopicella is worth trying. Bardolino is rarely interesting.	Good quality easy drinking wines that are generally reasonably priced.	Volume not quality is the motto here. Sangiovese di Romagna is one of the best wines.
Up to 8 years for best reds and whites of AA.	Valpolicella Classico: 3–5 Amarone: 4–10	Generally drink young.	Generally drink young.
–*	*–***	*–**	*–**
AA: Haas, Lageder, Tiefenbrunner; T: Ferrari, Mezzacorona, Simoncelli	So: Masi, Pieropan, Tedeschi; Val: Allegrini, Anselmi, Bertani, Masi, Quintarelli	Borgo del Tiglio, Collavini, Gravener, Jermann, Schiopetto	Fattoria Paradiso, Zerbina (Romangna); Fugazza (Piacentini)
93, 91, 90, 89	93. 90, 88, 86, 85, 83, 81, 79, 78, 77	n/a	n/a

CENTRAL ITALY
INCLUDING TUSCANY

REGION	TUSCANY	UMBRIA
Leading DOC and DOCGs	DOCG: Brunello di Montalcino (Brun), Carmignano Rosso, Chianti, Vernaccia di San Gimignano DOC: Pomino, Rosso di Montalcino, Rosso di Montepulciano	DOCG: Montefalco Sagrantino, Torgiano Riserva DOC: Montefalco, Orvieto, Torgiano
Climate	The hilly area gives a cooler, fresher and wetter climate in summer than that of Emilia-Romagna	Similar to Tuscany
Size (acres)	77,465	14,330
Avg. Vol. (gal.)	31.18 million	4.81 million
Chief grape varieties	Cabernet Sauvignon, Cabernet Franc, Canaiolo, Sangiovese (R) Chardonnay, Trebbiano, Vermentino, Vernaccia di San Gimignano (W)	Canaiolo, Sangiovese, Sarantino (R) Trebbiano (W)
Style	Vast range of styles even within a wine like Chianti, varying from a light easy drinking red to one that needs to age to show best.	Torgiano and Montefalco Sagrantino are full bodied reds that age well. Try the Montefalco Sagrantino Passito, a sweet red made from drying the grapes. Orvieto: dry tangy white; semi-sweet version (abboccato) is more honeyed but with crisp acidity.
Quality/buying tips	Some of Italy's best reds come from here, in particular Chianti Riveras, Brunello di Montalcino plus some of the super Vino da Tavolas (VDT). Few good whites except for occasional Chardonnay and Vernaccia di San Gimignano.	Umbria makes good Tuscan style reds. Orvieto best of whites especially abboccato.
Aging potential	Best reds 5–15+	5–10 reds
Price	**–****	**–***
Best producers	Brun: Altesino, Casanova di Neri, Costanti, Villa Banfi Chianti: Antinori, Capezzana, Castellare, Frescobaldi, Castello di Volpaia, Felsina Berardenga, Fontodi, Isole e Olena, Peppoli, Selvapiana, Vignamaggio, Villa di Vetrice VDT: Ornellaia, Sassicaia, Tignanello	Adanti, Antinori, Bigi, Caprai, Castello della Sala, Lungarotti
Best vintages	93, 91, 90, 88, 85, 83, 82, 79	93, 90, 88, 87, 85

MARCHES	ABRUZZO AND MOLISE	LAZIO
Rosso Conero, Rosso Piceno, Verdicchio dei Castelli di Jesi (W)	Montepulciano d'Abruzzo, Trebbiano d'Abruzzo	Frascati, Marino, Orvieto
Temperate but dry and hot in summer. Hillside sites are cooler	Best wines come from the cooler hillsides	Hot, dry summers
26,930	27,850	43,242
8.02 million	14.05 million	14.53 million
Montepulciano, Sangiovese (R) Trebbiano, Verdicchio (W)	Montepulciano (R) Trebbiano (W)	Aleatico, Sangiovese (R) Malvasia, Trebbiano (W)
Plummy, spicy mouthfilling reds. Crisp, slightly minerally whites.	Soft mouthfilling reds, bland whites.	Mainly white and rather bland. Orvieto: dry tangy white; semi-sweet version is more honeyed but with crisp acidity.
Reds tend to be the most interesting and are reasonably priced.	Reds can be most attractive chunky drinking. Whites not exciting.	Orvieto can be the best of the Lazio wines, especially the semi-sweet version. Frascati is not memorable. Marino, similar to Frascati is often better.
reds 2–6, whites drink young	2–6 (reds)	Best drunk young
**	**	*–**
Buscci, Fazi-Battaglia, Garofoli, Monte Schiavo, Umani Ronchi (San Lorenzo and Cumaro)	Illuminati, di Majo, Nicodemis, Cantina Tollo, Valentini, Ciccio Zaccagnani	Antinori, Colli Catone, Fontana Candida
93, 92, 91, 90, 89, 88	93, 92, 91, 90, 89, 88	n/a

SOUTHERN ITALY
AND THE ISLANDS

REGION	CAMPANIA	APULIA
Leading DOC and DOCGs	DOCG: Taurasi DOC: Vesuvio, Falerno di Massico	Aleatico di Puglia, Copertino, Locorotondo (R); Rosso Canosa, Salice Salentino (R/W)
Climate	Long hot, dry summer.	Long hot, dry summers. High day and night temperatures on plains where most vines are planted.
Size (acres)	2,965	39,240
Avg. Vol. (gal.)	1.15 million	4.72 million
Chief grape varieties	Asprinio, Fiano, Falanghuia, Greco (W) Aglianico, Sangiovese, Piedirosso (R)	Negroamaro, Primitivo (R) Chardonnay, Trebbiano (W)
Style	Taurasi is a concentrated and powerful red.	At their best the reds are deep colored, powerful and spicy.
Quality/buying tips	Taurasi is easily the best but needs aging. Rest of local interest.	Best wines from from Salento peninsula – Copertino and, in particular, Salice Salentino. Also Aleatico di Puglia, a red sweet, Muscat style, is worth trying.
Aging potential	Taurasi: 7–12	Copertino worth aging
Price	*–***	*–**
Best producers	Mastroberardino	Candido, Cantina Sociale Copertino, De Castris Taurino, Vallone
Best vintages	93, 92, 91, 90, 88, 86	93, 92, 91, 90, 89, 88

BASILICATA	CALABRIA	SICILY AND ISLANDS
Aglianico del Vulture	Ciró (R/W); Donnici, Savuto (R)	Marsala, Moscato di Pantelleria; otherwise no DOCs of importance
Hot dry summers but temperatures in mountainous areas considerably lower than on plains or coast.	Very hot, dry summers.	Very hot and dry.
3,373	14,330	54,360
248,330	914,565	3.41 million
Aglianico	Gaglioppo, Greco Nero (R) Greco Bianco, Malvasia (W)	Grillo, Inzolia, Trebbiano, Muscato (W) Calabrese, Nerello Mascalese, Perricone (R)
Powerful tannic but aromatic red that ages well.	Mainly robust reds.	Huge area. Modern technology and cooler hillside sites giving some crisp, lemony whites and powerful robust reds. Marsala (fortified) – dry to sweet.
One of Italy's best reds.	Although reds are best, these are wines to be drunk when in Calabria and nowhere else.	Improving area though patchy. Good quality Marsala is a revelation.
5–12	2–4	Best up to 6 years
***	*–**	*–***
Fratelli d'Angelo, Paternoster	Ceratti, Fattoria San Francesco	Corvo, Rincione; *Marsala*: De Bartoli, Florio, Pellegrino, Terre Arse
93, 92, 91, 90, 88, 87, 86, 85	93, 92, 91	94, 93, 92

NORTHERN ITALY

Many of Italy's most famous wines come from here: Asti Spumante, Barolo, Barbaresco, Soave, and Valpolicella. In Barolo and Barbaresco, the Italians have two fascinating and world-class wines that deserve to be better known.

CENTRAL ITALY

The central region is best known for the rolling hills of Tuscany with its Chianti and associated wines. However, it has other areas such as the Abruzzo, Marche, and Umbria which produce interesting wines which are well worth exploring.

SOUTHERN ITALY

The south is best known for making undistinguished bulk wine, especially in Apulia and Sicily. Sicily makes over 260 million gallons a year, yet little is classified as DOC. However, improvements are underway and reasonably priced, drinkable wines are emerging.

BELOW A sign for the Gallo Nero—a grouping of Chianti producers.

FRANCE

CALAIS

BELGIUM

LUXEMBOURG
GERMANY

⊕ VINEYARD AREA:
2.03 million acres

🍾 ANNUAL PRODUCTION:
1.37 billion gallons

🍷 ANNUAL CONSUMPTION
PER HEAD (GALLONS):
1973: 27.9
1993: 16.8

Champagne

STRASBOURG

PARIS

Marne

Alsace

ORLEANS

Chablis

DIJON

Côtes de
Beaune

Côtes de Nuits

SWITZERLAND

NANTES

Loire Valley

Cher

Loire

Chalonnais

Maconnais

Saône

Beaujolais

LYON

ITALY

Medoc

Blayais

Pomerol

St. Emilion

Dordogne

Rhône

Northern
Rhône

BORDEAUX

Entre Deux Mers

Graves

Sauternes

Garonne

Southern
Rhône

AVIGNON

Armagnac

TOULOUSE

Languedoc

MARSEILLE

Roussillon

SPAIN

VINEYARD AREA:
176,000 acres

ANNUAL PRODUCTION:
1.05 million gallons

BELOW *The dominating site of Sancerre and its vineyards.*

THE LOIRE

The Loire is a little over 600 miles long. The first vineyards are 530 miles from the ocean. However, vineyards of more than local interest begin at Pouilly, some 280 miles from the sea. The Loire has a remarkable diversity of wines in all three colors, still and sparkling, and of varying degrees of sweetness: from austerely dry to lusciously sweet.

Two grape varieties, Chenin Blanc and Cabernet Franc, come into their own in the Loire. Chenin Blanc, in particular, shows through the range of wines made from it that it is one of the world's most versatile varieties.

The easiest way of understanding Loire wines is by seeing how grape varieties change, as you travel downstream, to match the changes in climate. Sauvignon Blanc and Pinot Noir in the Central Vineyards of Sancerre and Pouilly gives way to Cabernet Franc and Chenin Blanc in Anjou and finally to Muscadet in Nantais vineyards close to the Atlantic.

ABOVE *The medieval town and château of Chinon—home of one of the Loire's best red wines, made almost entirely from Cabernet Franc.*

LEFT *Pouilly-sur-Loire: halfway down the 600 mile river. The vineyards now start in earnest.*

THE LOIRE

GRAPE VARIETY	SAUVIGNON BLANC	PINOT NOIR	GAMAY
Appellations	Sancerre (S), Pouilly-Fumé (PF), Menetou-Salon (M-S), Quincy (Q), Reuilly (R), Touraine (T)	St Pourçain, Sancerre (S), Menetou-Salon (M-S), Touraine (T)	Côtes de Forez, Roannaise, Auvergne Touraine (T), Anjou-Gamay (AG), Coteaux d'Ancenis
Soils	Chalk and limestone	Chalk and limestone	Chalk and limestone
Climate	Semi-Continental	Semi-Continental	Semi-Continental/semi-Oceanic
Size (acres)	n/a	n/a	n/a
Style/taste	Grassy, nettley, grapefruit	Raspberry and other berry fruits	Tangy berry fruit often with peppery spice
Aging potential	Pouilly-Fumé, Sancerre: up to 7 years	Sancerre: up to 5/6 years Menetou: 3/4 years	Best drunk within first 2 years
Quality/buying tips	A good Touraine Sauvignon is much better value than a cheap Sancerre	Can be very light and thin in poor years. Great years (89, 90) can be delicious	Often better value than Beaujolais
Best producers	S: Cotat, Bourgeois, Crochet, Mellot, Neveu; PF: Dagueneau, Ladoucette, Masson-Bondelet, Ch de Tracy; T: Delaunay, Oisly et Thésée	S: Bourgeois, Dezat, Natter, J.M. Roger, Vacheron; M-S: Pellé	T: Clos Roche-Blanche, Delaunay, Marionnet; AG: Daviau, Richou
Price	*—***	*—**	*—**
Best vintages	95, 94, 93, 90, 89, 88	95, 94, 93, 90, 89	95, 94, 93

CHENIN BLANC	CABERNET FRANC	MUSCADET (MELON DE BOURGOGNE)
Touraine-Amboise (TA), Touraine-Azay-le-Rideau (TAR), Montlouis (M), Vouvray (V), Jasnières (J), Saumur (S), Anjou (A), Savennières (SV), Coteaux du Layon (CL), Bonnezeaux (B), Quarts de Chaume (QC), Coteaux de l'Aubance (CA)	Touraine, Chinon (C), Bourgueil (B), St Nicolas de Bourgueil (StN), Saumur-Champigny (SC), Saumur (S), Anjou, Anjou Villages (AV)	Muscadet. Muscadet de Sèvre-et-Maine (MSM) Muscadet Coteaux de la Loire, (MC), Muscadet Côtes du Grand Lieu (MG)
Limestone/Schist	Limestone/Schist	Schist and granite
Semi-Continental/semi-Oceanic	Semi-Continental/semi-Oceanic	Oceanic
n/a	n/a	n/a
Huge range from very dry to luscious sweet	Blackcurrants, blackberries, green pepper, soot.	Lemony, hazelnut, yeasty, often quite neutral
Can live 100 years, esp. sweet wines from great years.	Best: 10–15 years.	Best producers 3–7 years.
Buy from a grower avoid négociants' brews	Again best from a producer rather than négociant	Worth spending bit extra for a *sur lie*
B: Angeli; CL: Baudouin, Cady, Papin, Ogereau, Pithon, Soulez; A: Baumard, Daviau, Orereau; QC: Baumard, Bellerive; V: Champalou, Foreau, Fouquet; SV: Closel, Epiré; CA: Daviau, Lébreton; SA: Huet	C: Baudry, Couly-Dutheil, Joguet; B: Breton, Druet; AV: Dariau, Lébreton, Ogereau, Richou; SC: Foucault, Val Brun, Vatan, Villeneuve; StN: Mabileau	MG: Batard, Bel Air, Choblet; MS: G. Bossard, Chereau-Carre, Guilbeau; Métaireau, Papin-Luneau, Sauvion; MC: Guindon
*–***	*–**	*–**
95, 94, 93, 90, 89, 88, 76, 59, 47, 21	95, 94, 93, 90, 89, 85, 76, 64, 59	95, 94, 94, 90, 82, 76

VINEYARD AREA:
273,446 acres (AC)

ANNUAL PRODUCTION: around 160 million gallons (approximately 80% red)

BORDEAUX

This the largest fine wine area in the world. There is a big range of wines from ordinary cheap Bordeaux red and white to some of the world's classiest estates and most expensive bottles. Estates with evocative names such as Cheval Blanc, Haut-Brion, Lafite, Pétrus, and d'Yquem have made Bordeaux's reputation. Along with Champagne, this is the vineyard with the closest ties to big business.

NORTH OF BORDEAUX: MÉDOC

The wines from the Médoc are predominantly red and Cabernet Sauvignon is the dominant grape variety with just over half the area planted. About a third is planted with Merlot, which is used to soften the tannic Cabernet Sauvignon. The best wines need to be aged, often for 10 years or more. However, modern winemaking techniques are emphasizing the fruit and this makes them drinkable much sooner than in the past.

WEST OF BORDEAUX: ST EMILLION/POMEROL, ETC.

The wines from Right Bank are predominantly red, excepting Blaye, which produces some white too. Here Merlot is the leading variety, generally producing softer wines that are usually ready to drink before those of the Médoc and Graves.

SOUTH OF BORDEAUX: GRAVES, SAUTERNES, BARSAC

Red wines continue but soon whites become increasingly important. This area produces the best dry whites of Bordeaux and, from Sauternes, some of the world's greatest sweet wines.

RIGHT *Château Guirand—a top Sauternes estate and now Canadian owned.*

RIGHT *Château Tayac, Côtes de Blaye—not quite the same class as Mouton and without the same financial means.*

BELOW *The gravelly vineyards of Château Latour, Pauillac. The château and the famous tower are in the background.*

BOTTOM *Château Mouton-Rothschild—the very impressive barrel Chai, Pauillac, France.*

BORDEAUX
THE LEFT BANK – MÉDOC

VILLAGE/AC	HAUT-MÉDOC	MARGAUX	ST JULIEN
Chief grapes	Cabernet Sauvignon/Merlot	Cabernet Sauvignon/Merlot	Cabernet Sauvignon/Merlot
Size (acres)	9,637	3,237	2,214
Avg. Vol. (gal.)	5.81 million	1.85 million	977,466
Soils	Gravel	Gravel	Gravel
Climate	Temperate Oceanic often with fine fall weather.	Temperate Oceanic often with fine fall weather.	Temperate Oceanic often with fine fall weather.
Style	Wide variations: but often marked by spicy blackcurrant fruit.	Softer, more opulent and more perfumed than other Médocs.	Combines the soft appeal of Margaux with the more austere Pauillacs.
Quality/buying tips	Some bargains to be had.	The big names can be variable.	High quality, be suspicious of cheap bottles.
Aging potential	4–25	5–40+	5–40+
Best producers	Cantermerle, Cissac, La Lagune, Lamarque, Lanessan	d'Angludet, Giscours, d'Issan, Lascombes, Margaux, Palmer, Siran	Beychevelle, Ducru-Beaucaillou, Gruard Larose, Leoville-Barton, Leoville-Les Cases, Talbot
Price	*–***	**–****	**–****
Best vintages	95, 94, 90, 89, 88, 86, 85, 83, 82, 78, 76, 70, 66, 61, 59	95, 94, 90, 89, 88, 86, 85, 83, 82, 78, 76, 70, 66, 61, 59	95, 94, 90, 89, 88, 86, 85, 83, 82, 78, 76, 70, 66, 61, 59

The wines from the Médoc are predominantly red and Cabernet Sauvignon is the principal grape.

PAUILLAC	ST ESTÈPHE	MOULIS/LISTRAC	MÉDOC
Cabernet Sauvignon	Cabernet Sauvignon/Merlot	Cabernet Sauvignon/Merlot	Merlot
2,805	3,015	1,188 (M); 1,900 (L)	1,038
1.53 million	1.85 million	792,500; 1 million	2.75 million
Gravel	Gravel	Gravel, clay and limestone	Sand/gravel
Temperate Oceanic often with fine fall weather.	Temperate Oceanic often with fine fall weather.	Temperate Oceanic often with fine fall weather.	Temperate Oceanic often with fine fall weather.
Often markedly blackcurrant, plus cigar-box and pencil shavings with maturity.	Austere, tannic wines that often need long aging to show best.	Soft concentration of berry fruit.	At their best softer, ready to drink sooner.
High quality, be suspicious of cheap bottles.	Generally high but quality is more variable than St Julien.	Good quality and value. Some bargains to be had.	Some bargains to be had but rarely the tops.
5–50+	6–40+	3–25	3–20
Batailley, Haut-Batailley, Lafite, Latour, Lynch-Bages, Mouton-Rothschild, Pichon-Longueville, Pichon-Longueville-Lalande	Cos d'Estournel, Lafon-Rochet, Lilian Ladouys, Montrose, Ormes de Pez	Chasse-Spleen, Maucaillou, Poujeaux	la Cardonne, Potensac, Tour-de-By, Tour-St-Bonnet
–**	**–****	**–***	*–**
95, 94, 90, 89, 88, 86, 85, 83, 82, 78, 76, 70, 66, 61, 59, 45	95, 94, 90, 89, 88, 86, 85, 83, 82, 78, 76, 70, 66, 61, 59	95, 94, 90, 89, 88, 86, 85, 83, 82, 78	95, 94, 90, 89, 88, 86, 85

BORDEAUX
RIGHT BANK: POMEROL AND SAINT-EMILION

VILLAGE/AC	POMEROL/LALANDE DE POMEROL (LdeP)	ST EMILION	OTHER ST EMILION APPELLATIONS*
Chief grapes	Merlot (Cabernet Franc)	Merlot Cabernet Franc, (Cabernet Sauvignon)	Merlot, Cabernet Franc
Size (acres)	1,878; LdeP: 2,660	13,100	9,316
Avg. Vol. (gal.)	1 million LdeP: 1.45 million	7.4 million	7.13 million
Soils	Clay, gravel, sand	Côtes (around the town of St Emilion: limestone). Gravel on plateau west of town.	Very varied
Style/taste	At its best opulently rich plummy fruit.	Similar soft plummy fruit.	Similarly soft wines to StE but lighter and less structured.
Quality/buying tips	Pomerol is pricey because it is the most fashionable Bordeaux appellation. Lalande can be good value.	Because of the high proportion of Merlot and small amount of Cabernet Sauvignon used these wines mature more quickly than the Médoc.	Lower priced than St Emilion and Pomerol, some bargains to be had.
Aging potential	8–35+	5–30+	3–20
Best producers	Beauregard, L'Enclos, L'Evangile, Pétrus, Vieux Château Certain LdeP: Grand Ormeau, Real-Caillou	Angelus, Ausone, Cheval Blanc, Canon, Figeac, Magdelaine, Monbousquet, Tertre Rôteboeuf	La Grenière, Lion Perruchon, Maison Blanche, Vieux Chateau Saint Andre, St Georges
Price	***–**** (** LdeP)	**–****	**
Best vintages	94, 93, 90, 89, 88, 86, 85, 83, 82, 81, 79, 78, 76, 75	94, 93, 90, 89, 88, 86, 85, 83, 82, 81, 79, 78, 76, 75	94, 93, 90, 89, 88, 86, 85

*: The other appellations of St Emilion are: Lussac, Montagne, Puisseguin, St Georges.

The wines from Right Bank are predominantly red, excepting Blaye which produces some white too. Here Merlot is the leading variety, generally producing softer wines that are usually ready to drink before those of the Médoc and Graves. It has a broadly Oceanic climate similar to the rest of Bordeaux, although rather cooler soils than the Médoc.

FRONSAC/CANON FRONSAC	CÔTES DE CASTILLON, CÔTES DE FRANCS	BLAYE/PREMIÈRES CÔTES DE BLAYE	BOURG/CÔTES DE BOURG
Merlot, Cabernet Franc (Malbec, Cabernet Sauvignon)	Merlot, Cabernet Franc (Malbec, Cabernet Sauvignon)	R: Merlot, Cabernet Sauvignon W: Colombard, Sauvignon, Ugni Blanc	as Blaye
2,760	7,480	9,640	8,800
1.45 million Fronsac: 1.08 million	4.23 million	6.08 million (R: 5.5 million, W: 508,000)	5.34 million (R: 5.28 million, W: 47,550)
Limestone/sandstone	Clay-limestone	Very varied	Clay-limestone
Quite powerful, full bodied reds that can age well.	Often soft berry fruit reds.	Generally quite light easy-drinking reds.	More full-bodied than Blaye.
Improving quality makes this area worth searching out.	Improving quality makes this area worth searching out.	There are bargains to be had in AC Premières Côtes de Blaye.	Some increasingly good reds at fair prices.
3–15	3–15	2–10	2–10
Moulin-Haut-Laroque, Moulin Pey-Labrie, Vrai Canon Bouche	Castillon: de Belcier, de Pitray Francs: Francs, Puyguerand	Bertinière, Haut-Terrier, Segonzac	de Barbe, Macay, Tayac
**	*–**	*–**	*–**
94, 93, 90, 89, 88, 86, 85	94, 93, 90, 89, 88, 86, 85	94, 93, 90, 89	94, 93, 90, 89

BORDEAUX
GRAVES AND SAUTERNES AREA PLUS REGIONAL BORDEAUX ACs

VILLAGE/ APPELLATION	PESSAC-LÉOGNAN	GRAVES	BARSAC	SAUTERNES
Chief grapes	Sémillon, Sauvignon (W); Cabernet Sauvignon, Merlot, Cabernet Franc (R)	Sémillon, Sauvignon (W); Cabernet Sauvignon, Merlot, Cabernet Franc (R)	Sémillon, Sauvignon, Muscadelle	Sémillon, Sauvignon, Muscadelle
Size (acres)	2,696 (R: 2,132, W: 563)	6,670 (R: 4,448, W: 2,222)	1,554	3,637
Avg. Vol. (gal.)	1.61 million (R: 1.27 million, W: 343,000)	3.75 million (R: 2.54 million, W: 1.22 million)	356,643	660,450 (varies greatly from year to year)
Soils	Gravel	Gravel	Sand and limestone	Diverse: gravel, clay-limestone, limestone
Climate	Temperate oceanic often with fine fall weather.	Temperate oceanic often with fine fall weather.	Similar to Graves but with fall mist from River Ciron.	(As Barsac)
Style	Well structured reds, often with a mineral and smoky character. Complex, long-lasting whites.	Similar in style to Pessac but lighter, less long-lasting wines (R&W)	Similar in style to Sauternes but usually a little lighter.	At best lusciously sweet with complex flavors of dried fruits.
Quality/buying tips	Best dry white and red vineyards south of Bordeaux.	While not of the quality of Pessac-Léognan, these can be good value.	Like Sauternes buy best you can afford and from a good vintage.	Good sweet wines are expensive – buy the best you can afford.
Aging potential	10–40+	5–25	15–70+	20–75+
Best producers	Chevalier, Fieuzal, Haut-Brion, Larrivet-Haut-Brion, Laville-Haut-Brion (W), La Louvière, Malartic-Lagravière, Pape Clement, la Tour Martillac	Carbonnieux, Ferrande, Clos Floridène, Rahoul	Climens, Coutet, Doisy-Daëne, Nairac	Bastor-Lamontagne, Guiraud, Lafaurie-Peyraguey, Raymond-Lafon, Suduiraut, d'Yquem
Price	***–****	**–***	**–***	**–****
Best vintages	94, 90, 89, 88, 86, 85, 83, 82, 78, 70, 66, 61 (W)	94, 90, 89, 88, 86, 85, 83, 82 (W)	90, 89, 88, 86, 83, 76, 71, 70, 67, 59, 47	90, 89, 88, 86, 85, 83, 76, 71, 70, 67, 59, 47, 21

Vineyards to the south of Bordeaux and producing the most varied wines in the region.

ST CROIX DE MONT, CADILLAC, CERONS, LOUPIAC	ENTRE-DEUX-MERS	BORDEAUX/ BORDEAUX SEC	PREMIÈRES CÔTES DE BORDEAUX
Sémillon, Sauvignon, Muscadelle	Sauvignon, Sémillon	Cabernet Sauvignon, Cabernet Franc, Merlot, Malbec, Petit Verdot, Carmenère (R); Sauvignon, Sémillon, Muscadelle (W)	As Bordeaux
2,460	6,180	141, 415 (R: 113,960, W: 27,455)	7,228 (R: 5,868, SW: 1,360)
861,227	3.96 million	n/a	3.9 million (R: 3.21 million, SW: 686,868)
Chalk, gravel	Clay and sand	Very diverse	Very diverse
Similar but fewer fall mists.			
Similar in style to Sauternes but less rich.	Increasingly Sauvignon dominated. Some good crisp wines but still too many flabby boring ones.	Reds: the best are well made with soft easy fruit. At worst: thin, tannic and dreary. Whites: as Entre Deux Mers.	Attractively, soft fruity reds as well as lightly honeyed sweet wines.
Very variable quality but can be very good value.	Very variable quality but can be very good value.	At its best offers good value. But there are still too many drab, boring fruitless wines.	Increasingly well made (R) Can be good value (SW).
3–20	Drink young	R: 2–5, W: Drink young	2–5
Cerons: de Cérons, Fayau; St Croix de Mont: du Mont; Loupiac: du Noble, de Ricaud (L)	Bonnet, Ducla, La Lezardiève	Bonnet, Crabitan-Bellevue, Fayau, Gardera, de Lyne, Penin, Reynon, Sours, Timberlay, Thieuley, Tour de Mirabeau	de Berbec, de Chelivette, Plaisance, Reynon
**	**	*–**	**
90, 89, 88, 86, 83	94, 93	94, 93	94, 93, 90, 89

VINEYARD AREA:
180,000 acres

ANNUAL PRODUCTION:
1.22 million gallons

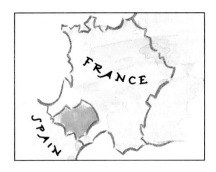

SOUTHWEST FRANCE

Although some of these widespread vineyards are only a hundred miles from Bordeaux, they are far removed from the big money of Bordeaux. In a world where many wines are increasingly bland and restricted to a small number of international varieties, Southwest France makes characterful wines from unusual varieties. The area is well worth exploring.

There is a wide range of styles. The best reds which come from Cahors and Madiran are robust and powerful. They go well with the region's rich food. The reds from Buzet and Bergerac are more in the lighter, Bordeaux style. Jurançon, in the foothills of the Pyrenees around the attractive town of Pau, is the most interesting of the whites. The best have a thrilling balance of fruit and acidity. Farther north are the sweet wines of Monbazillac, which although uneven in quality, can be a deliciously honeyed bargain as they are much cheaper than Sauternes.

ABOVE *Cahors: the meandering sweep of the River Lot and its vineyards which produce some of the region's best red wines.*

RIGHT *The tiny but atmospheric vineyards of Irouléguy in the foothills of the Western Pyrenees. At the end of World War II they were close to extinction, but are now enjoying revived fortunes.*

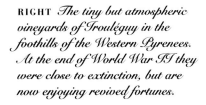

VINEYARD AREA:
805,000 acres

ANNUAL PRODUCTION:
5.4 million gallons

ABOVE *The last two decades have seen the rebirth of quality wine production on the often inhospitable hillsides of Languedoc.*

LANGUEDOC-ROUSSILLON

It is amazing that France, which has been growing grapes and making wine for thousands of years, should have one of the world's most exciting and dynamic vineyards. For 150 years the Midi specialized in producing rough wines. In the last twenty years that has changed and there are now vignerons who are now producing stunningly good wines, both as Appellation Contrôlée wines and in the increasingly important *vins de pays* category.

The vineyards of Languedoc-Roussillon stretch from the gates of Avignon and the fascinating Camargue Delta down to the Spanish border where the Pyrenees meets the Mediterranean at Banyuls.

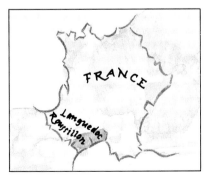

RIGHT *The picturesque Mediterranean port and resort of Collioure, close to the Spanish border. The vineyards produce both Collioure and Banyuls.*

LANGUEDOC-ROUSSILLON
APPELLATIONS AND VIN DE PAYS: LANGUEDOC

APPELLATION/TYPE	COSTIÈRES DE NÎMES (CdeN)	COTEAUX DU LANGUEDOC	FAUGÈRES (F)/ ST CHINIAN (StC)
Cru or sub region or AC for VDN and Limoux		La Clape, Montpeyroux, Picpoul de Pinet, Pic St Loup, St Christol	
Size (acres)	29,650	15,567	F: 3,460 StC: 4,942
Avg. Vol. (gal.)	3.96 million (75%: R, 22%: Ro, 3%: W)	9.25 million	F: 1.59 million StC: 2.19 million
Soils	River-borne stones	Very varied: gravel, schist, limestone	F: Schist StC: Schist/limestone
Grapes	Carignan, Cinsault, Counoise, Grenache, Mourvèdre, Syrah (R); Clairette, Grenache Bl, Maccabéo, Marsanne, Rolle, Rousanne, Ugni Blanc (W)	Picpoul (W), otherwise similar to CdeN	Carignan, Syrah, Mourvèdre, Grenache, Cinsault
Style	Reds are attractively round and soft	Range from light and fruity to concentrated wines needing time	Often full-bodied spicy reds. The best need to age
Quality/buying tips	Big improvements in quality over last 5 years. Worth trying	The best is very exciting and excellent value. But there is still too much poor wine	Among the best reds from the Midi
Aging potential	2–8	2–8	3–10
Price	*–**	*–**	*–***
Best producers	Beaubois, Campuget, Mas Carlot, Mourgues du Gres, du Rosier, de la Tuilerie, Tourelles	Calage, Feline – Jourdan (W), La Coste, Hortus, Jullien, Mas Brugière, Mire l'Etang, Pech Redon, Peyre Rose, la Roque, Valmagne	F: Alquier, Estanilles, Fraisse, Grezan, Roque; StC: Bagatelle, Berlou, Cazal Viel, Maurel Fonsalade
Best vintages	95, 94, 93, 91, 90, 89, 88	95, 94, 93, 91, 90, 89, 88	95, 94, 93, 91, 90, 89, 88

†: Includes Rouissillon   ††: VDQS

MINERVOIS (M)/ CORBIÈRES (C)/FITOU (F)	LIMOUX (L), CABARDÈS††(C) CÔTES DE MALEPÈRE††(M)	VINS DE PAYS†	VIN DOUX NATUREL
	Blanquette de Limoux, Crémant de Limoux	Aude, Côtes Catalanes, Herault, d'Oc, Pyrenees-Orientales	Muscat de Frontignan, Muscat de Lunel, Muscat de Mireval, Muscat de St Jean de Minervois
M:11,120 C: 34,594 F: 4,942	C: 5,436	n/a	3,531
M: 7.0 million C: 13.21 million F: 2.38 million	C: 396,270 M: 792,540	2.64 million	1.28 million
Very varied – sand to limestone	Limestone and other soils	Very varied	Very varied
Similar to Faugères	Chardonnay, Chenin Blanc, Mauzac (W); Carignan, Syrah, Mourvèdre, Grenache, Cinsault, Cabernet Sauvignon, Merlot (R)	Cabernet Sauvignon, Chardonnay, Malbec, Merlot, Muscat, Sauvignon, Syrah, Viognier, and others	Muscat
Big ranges of styles from light gulping reds to full-bodied spicy wines	Fine Chardonnay: Limoux	Vast range of styles	Always sweet. New style are fresh with critric and marmalade flavors. Old style: oxidized and heavy
Often good value. The 94 vintage is particularly good	Limoux makes the best Chardonnay in the Midi, sparklers are good too. Reds less so	Variable quality but best offer excellent value	Can often be better value than Muscat Beaumes de Venise
3–10	2–5	Up to 5	Best drunk young
*–**	*–**	*–***	*–***
C: Baillat, Amouries, Lastours, Ollieux, Palais, Parc, St Auriol, Voulte Gasparets, Bories-Azeau; F: Mont Tauch; M: Domergue, Gourgazaud, La Livinière, Tour Boisèe	L: l'Aigle, Delmas, Sieur d'Arques C: Ventenac, Salitis M: Montlaur, Routier	L'Aigle, Capion, Chemins de Bassac, Herrick, Hardy, Laporte, Mas Cremat, Mas de Daumas Gassac, Puig, Rectorie, Raissac, St Hilaire, Schistes, Sieur d'Arques, Terre Megre, Vacquier	St Jean: de Barroubio, Vignerons de Septimanie; Lunel: Capelle
95, 94, 93, 91, 90, 89, 88	95, 94, 93, 91, 90, 89	95, 94, 93	95, 94, 93

LANGUEDOC-ROUSSILLON
APPELLATIONS AND VIN DE PAYS: ROUSSILLON

APPELLATION/TYPE	CÔTES DU ROUSSILLON/ CÔTES DU ROUSSILLON VILLAGES *(red only)*	COLLIOURE	VIN DOUX NATUREL
Cru or sub region or AC for VDN	Caramany, Latour de France	as above	Banyuls (B), Maury (M), Muscat de Rivesaltes (MdeR), Rivesaltes (R)
Size (acres)	13,343	815	58,328
Avg. Vol. (gal.)	8.45 million	264,180	14.08 million
Soils	Schist/limestone	Schist	Schist/limestone
Grapes	Carignan, Cinsault, Grenache, Mourvèdre, Syrah, W: Clairette, Grenache Bl, Maccabéo, Marsanne, Rolle, Rousanne, Ugni Blanc	Carignan, Cinsault, Counoise, Grenache, Mourvèdre, Syrah	Carignan, Grenache, Muscat
Style	Fast-improving reds, most whites still uninspired.	Powerful, mouthfilling red which can age well.	Range of flavors from cherries to raisins, coffee, and chocolate.
Quality/buying tips	Reds offer good value.	Quite expensive, often difficult to find but can be the best red of Roussillon.	Very variable but at its best one of the great fortified wines of the world.
Aging potential	2–6	3–10	2–30
Price	*–**	**–***	*–***
Best producers	Casenove, Cazes, Gauby, Sarda-Malet, Vignerons de Maury, Mas Cremat, Domaine des Chênes	Casa Blanca, Mas Blanc, La Rectorie, La Tour Vieille, Templiers	B: Casa Blanca, L'Etoile, Mas Blanc, La Rectorie, La Tour Vieille, Templiers. M: Mas Amiel, Pléiade, Vignerons de Maury R&MdeR: Cazes, Laporte, Puig
Best vintages	94, 93, 91, 90, 89, 88	94, 93, 91, 90, 89, 88	94, 93, 90, 89, 88, 85, 82, 78, 73, 63

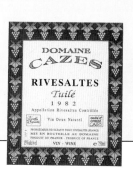

VINEYARD AREA:
28,328 acres

ANNUAL PRODUCTION:
845,353 gallons

RIGHT *Vineyard of Mas de la Dame, Les Baux-de-Provence, Bouches-du-Rhône, France.*

THE RHÔNE VALLEY

SOUTHERN RHÔNE AND PROVENCE

Down at the end of the Rhône Valley the climate and the vegetation are markedly different from the northern Rhône. This is Mediterranean France, with its characteristic white walls, summer heat, mistral blasts, and continuous dry chirruping of the crickets. Here at the foot of the Rhône and eastward around the coast toward the Italian border are some of the oldest vineyards of France. The Greeks first planted vines near Marseilles back in the sixth century B.C.

Much of the wine made in Provence goes to lubricate the throats of the summer throng on the Côte d'Azur. However, standards have improved and there is more to the wines of the area than pleasantly alcoholic Côtes de Provence rosé. Three of the most interesting areas are Bandol, which makes long lived reds from Mourvèdre just west of Toulon, and the Coteaux d'Aix and Coteaux des Baux further inland. The two Coteaux appellations produce impressive reds from a blend of Cabernet Sauvignon and traditional Mediterranean varieties.

NORTHERN RHÔNE

South of Lyon the narrow Rhône Valley corridor funnels travelers past a number of evocatively named vineyards such as Côte Rotie (the roasted slope) and Hermitage. The vineyards are perched on the steep slopes crisscrossed with terraces to try to keep the vines and the soil in place. Production is limited and these wines are now fashionable, so prices have risen accordingly.

NORTHERN RHÔNE

APPELLATION	CÔTE ROTIE (R)	CONDRIEU (W)	CHÂTEAU-GRILLET (W)	HERMITAGE (R, W)
Size (acres)	373	148	7.4	311
Avg. Vol. (gal.)	118,800	31,173	2,377	132,090
Soils	Limestone, clay and slate	Mica, schist	Granite	Granite
Grapes	Syrah Viognier (max 20%)	Viognier	Viognier	Roussanne Marsanne; Syrah
Style	Raspberry, violets – mix of power and delicacy. Less massive than Hermitage.	Rich, full wine often with aromas and flavors of apricot.	Exotically floral aromas, mouthfilling fruit.	Powerful deep-colored reds, full-bodied whites.
Quality	Generally good especially from established producers.	Variable but at its best can be intensely perfumed.	Highly priced, sadly quality does not always match price.	Can be among the best reds in France. Powerful wine needing aging.
Aging potential	4–12	Usually best drunk young	3–7	5–20+
Price	***	***	****	***
Best producers	Barge, Rostang, Champet, Guigal, Jamet, Jasmin	Cuilleron, Perret, Dumazet, Guigal, Rozay, Vernay	Neyrat-Gachet (sole producer)	Chapoutier, Chave, Grippat, Jaboulet, Sorrel, Faure, Viale
Best vintages	94, 91, 90, 89, 88, 85	94	92, 91, 90, 89	94, 91, 90, 89, 88, 85

CROZES-HERMITAGE (R, W)	ST JOSEPH (R, W)	ST PÉRAY (Sp, W)	CORNAS (R)
2,543	1,606	143	185
1.06 million	581,196	66,045	79,250
Similar to Hermitage but richer soils	Granite	Granite	Granite, clay, sand
Roussanne Marsanne; Syrah	Roussanne Marsanne; Syrah	Marsanne Roussanne	Syrah
At their best similar to Hermitage though less powerful.	Deep-colored chewy reds but ready to drink sooner than Hermitage.	Rather heavy, white fizz.	Very deep reds – nearly black. Powerful; time to soften tannins.
Young wine-makers are rapidly improving quality and image.	Variable quality but from a good producer can be region's best value.	Rarely seen outside region.	The most powerful and tannic of the region's reds. Needs to age.
4–10	2–8	n/a	5–15
**	**	**	**—***
Fayolle, Graillot, Jaboulet	Chave, Florentin, Gonon, Grippat, Gripa	Fauterie	Clape, Lionnet, Michel, Verset, Colombo
94, 91, 90, 89, 88, 85	94, 91, 90, 89, 88	n/a	91, 90, 89, 88, 85

SOUTHERN RHÔNE

The region produces a wide variety of wines in all three colors including the popular fortified sweet wine,
Muscat Beaumes de Venise

Appellation	Côtes du Rhône/Côtes du Rhône Villages	Gigondas (G)/Lirac (L)/Vacqueyras (V)	Châteauneuf-du-Pape	Tavel
Size (acres)	10,872/9,884	2,965/1,186/1,729	7,907	2,347
Avg. Vol. (gal.)	58.12 million/ 3.96 million	1.08 million/501,900/ 660,450	2.64 million	1.11 million
Soils	Large area with very varied soils	Limestone and clay	Large round stones borne by the Rhône	Chalk and sand
Chief grapes	Grenache, Cinsault, Syrah, Mourvèdre	Grenache, Syrah, Mourvèdre, Cinsault	Grenache, Mourvèdre, Syrah	Grenache, Cinsault
Style	Varies from soft juicy, easy drinking reds to powerfully structured ones. Some whites and rosés.	Gigondas and Vacqueyras are powerful, soft spicy reds. Lirac is similar but less full-bodied.	Powerful reds, full-bodied, spice, and tobacco. Small amount of powerful, full-flavored white.	Rosé only – quite heady, full-bodied.
Quality/buying tips	Very variable, the best can be delicious.	From an individual estate these can be very good value. Gigondas can age well.	Beware of anonymous bottles, buy an estate bottled – will always have crest on bottle.	Can be one of France's best rosés.
Aging potential	2–8	3–12	5–20	Reputed to age well but I don't agree
Price	*–**	**–***	**–***	**
Best producers	Coudoulet de Beaucastel, Guigal, Remejeanne, Trignon/Alary, Combe, Rabasse Charavin, Ste-Anne	G: Longue-Toque, Pallières, Raspail, St Gayan; L: Cantegril-Verda, Fermade, La Mordurée; V: Clos de Cazaux, Couralou, Fourmone, Garrigue, Lambertins	Beaucastel, Clos des Papes, Font de Michelle, Mont Redon, Nalys, la Nerthe, Vieux Télégraphe	d'Aquéria, Genestière, Maby, Genestière, Mordorée
Best vintages	94, 90, 89, 88	94, 90, 89, 88, 85	94, 90, 89, 88, 85, 78	Drink young

VINEYARD AREA:
47,348 acres

ANNUAL PRODUCTION:
766,207 gallons

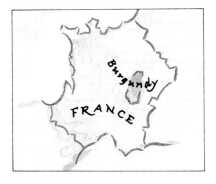

BURGUNDY

Bordeaux may impress through its wealth and the succession of fine properties with their imposing buildings, but Burgundy appeals to the senses. Burgundy has romance. It is a much more sensuous wine. Burgundy is for lovers of good living. It is a wine for lovers. One of Burgundy's most famous vineyards is called Les Amoureuses. Such a name would be inconceivable in Bordeaux!

Of course as with all love affairs there is the possibility of terrible disappointments. This is compounded by the fragmented pattern of vineyard ownership. Unlike Bordeaux there are no large estates, just a complex patchwork of ownership.

RIGHT *Château de Rully—a leading estate in the Côte Chalonnaise.*

RIGHT *A marker stone for Richebourg vineyard at Vosne-Romanée.*

BURGUNDY
CÔTE DE BEAUNE, CHALONNAIS, MACONNAIS, BEAUJOLAIS

REGION	CÔTE DE BEAUNE	CÔTE DE BEAUNE
Appellation	Ladoix (L), Pernand-Vergelesses (PV), Aloxe-Corton†(AC), Savigny-les-Beaune (SV), Chorey-les-Beaune (Ch), Pommard (PM), Volnay (VN)	Montélie (Mt), St-Romain (StR), Auxey-Duresses, Meursault (Mr), St-Aubin (StA), Puligny-Montrachet†(PM), Chassagne-Montrachet†(CM), Santenay (Snt)
Size (acres)	Ladoix: 227; Pernand-Vergelesses: 284; Aloxe-Corton†: 674; Savigny-les-Beaune: 842; Chorey-les-Beaune: 314; Pommard: 780; Volnay: 551	Montélie: 284; St-Romain: 198; Auxey-Duresses: 331; Meursault: 922; St-Aubin: 341; Puligny-Montrachet: 603; Chassagne-Montrachet: 729; Santenay: 764
Avg. Vol. (gal.)	Total – Côte de Beaune: 4.44 million	n/a
Soils	Limestone and marls	Limestone and marls
Grapes	Pinot Noir, Chardonnay	Chardonnay, Pinot Noir
Style	Powerful, complex, elegantly opulent reds. Whites less important except for the great rich buttery Corton-Charlemagne.	Whites to the fore especially in Meursault and the Montrachet villages. Powerful concentrated whites. Reds have less intensity than Volnay, Pommard and Corton.
Quality/buying tips	Many of the best reds from the Côte de Beaune come from these villages. Savigny can be good value.	Produces some of the greatest Chardonnay/white wine in the world plus some fine reds. Lesser known villages like St Romain and St Aubin offer value.
Price	***–****	***–****
Best producers	L: Chevalier, Cornu, Maillard PV: Bonneau du Martray, Germain, Rollin; AC: Bonneau du Martray, Jadot, Latour, Rapet, Tollot-Beaut, SV: Bize, Ecard, Maréchal, Tollot-Beaut; Ch: Drouhin, Germain; PM: Clerget, de Montille, Mussy; VN: Clerget, Lafarge, Lafon, de Montille, Poussé d'Or	Mt: Leflaive, Leroy, Olivier, Roulot, Suremain; StR: Bazenet, Charton et Truchet, Jaffelin; Mr: Ampeau, Coche-Dury, Lafon, Morey, Roulet: StA: Germain, Jadot, Lamy, Roux; PM: Carillon, Chartron, Colin, Drouhin, Leflaive, Laguiche, Ramonet, Sauzet; CM: Duc de Magenta, Gagnard, Lamy, Morey; Snt: Colin, Girardin, Morey, Poussé d'Or, Roux
Best Vintages	W: 93, 92, 90, 89, 88, 86, 85, 81, 79, 78, 72, 71 R: 92, 90, 89, 88, 85, 83, 78, 71	W: 93, 92, 90, 89, 88, 86, 85, 81, 79, 78 R: 92, 90, 89, 88, 85, 83

† *has Grand Cru vineyards*

CÔTE CHALONNAISE	MÂCONNAIS	BEAUJOLAIS*
Bouzeron, Côte Chalonnaise, Givry, Mercurey, Montagny, Rully	Mâcon (M), Mâcon Villages, Pouilly-Fuissé (PF), Pouilly-Loché, Pouilly-Vinzelles	Beaujolais, Beaujolais Villages, St Amour, Julienas, Chenas, Fleurie, Moulin à Vent, Chiroubles, Morgon
2,965	12,010	44,725
1.56 million	8.73 million	35.67 million
Limestone	Limestone	Schist and granite; limestone in southern Beaujolais
Aligoté, Chardonnay, Pinot Noir	Chardonnay, Gamay, Pinot Noir	Gamay, (Chardonnay)
Lighter versions of the reds and whites from the Côte de Beaune to the north.	Mâcon Villages: white only. The best Pouillys are rich buttery Chardonnays. Much Mâcon red and white is bland and boring.	Juicy easy drinking reds except for some of the Crus like Moulin à Vent or Morgon which are a bit more full-bodied.
The Chalonnais offers very good value in comparison to the better known Côte d'Or, especially from the individual villages such as Givry, Mercuey.	Sadly wines from the Mâconnais are rarely exciting but often are over priced. Look out for a known producer. **Avoid** anonymous bottles. Pouilly can be very good but again choose carefully.	Unfortunately very variable. Can be deliciously gulpable or thin cherry pop.
–*	**–***	*–**
Cave de Buxy, Derain, Faiveley, Juillot, Rodet, de Villaine, Bouchard Père et Fils, Sarrazin, Suremain, Thénard	M: Baudiers, Manciat-Poncet, Thévenet, Co-ops: Classé, Prissé, Viré PF: Coron, Corsin, Denogent, Feret, Ch. Fuissé, Lassarat	Cellier des Samsons, Duboeuf, Fessy, Ch de Juliénas, Ch du Moulin à Vent, Pelletier
93, 92, 91, 90, 89, 88, 86, 85	93, 92, 91, 90, 89, 88	94, 93, 91, 89, 88

* Beaujolais Crus (St Amour etc.) listed from north to south

BURGUNDY
CHABLIS AND CÔTES DE NUITS

REGION	YONNE	YONNE (Cont)	BOURGOGNE (REGIONAL ACs)
Appellations	Petit Chablis, Chablis, Chablis Premier Cru, Chablis Grand Cru	Côte d'Auxerre, Irancy (I), Sauvignon de St Bris (SB)	Bourgogne, Bourgogne Aligoté, Bourgogne Passetoutgrains, Crémant de Bourgogne
Size (acres)	Petit Chablis: 741, Chablis: 6,178, Chablis Premier Cru: 1,730, Chablis Grand Cru: 222	Côte d'Auxerre: 400, Irancy: 277, Sauvignon de St Bris: 166	Bourgogne: 8,112, Bourgogne Aligoté: 2,525, Bourgogne Passetoutgrains: 2,985, Crémant de Bourgogne: 940
Avg. Vol. (gal.)	Petit Chablis: 396,270, Chablis: 2.91 million, Chablis Premier Cru: 1.06 million, Chablis Grand Cru: 138,695	Côte d'Auxerre: 2,377 Irancy: 158,500, Sauvignon de St Bris: 118,800	Total: 9.97 million
Soils	Kimmeridgian limestone and clay	(same)	Various: mainly limestone
Climate	Semi-Continental: cold winters, spring frosts	(same)	(same)
Grapes	Chardonnay	Chardonnay, Pinot Noir, Sauvignon	Aligoté, Chardonnay, Gamay, Pinot Noir
Style	White. Classically lemon, minerally austerity with Premier and Grand Cru being more concentrated.	Grassy, quite full Sauvignons, Chardonnay similar in style to Chablis. Light reds.	Reds: Berry fruit especially raspberry. Whites: Aligoté: lemony fresh; Chardonnay: not same weight and power as those in Côte de Beaune.
Quality/buying tips	Buy from a known producer and oaked Chablis is usually best avoided.	The Chardonnays can offer a reasonably priced alternative to Chablis but small production.	Can be good value and the closest thing to an inexpensive Burgundy.
Aging potential	Good Premier and Grand Cru **need** aging: Premier 3–7 years, Grand: 5–20 years	2–5. Generally wines to be drunk young	2–4. Generally wines to be drunk young, especially Aligoté
Price	**–***	**	**
Best producers	Brocard, La Chablisenne, Dauvissat, Defaix, Durup, Laroche, Légland, Michel, Moreau, Raveneau, Vocoret	I: Brocard, Colinot, Delaloge; SB: Goisot, Renard	Cave de Buxy, Cave de Hautes Côtes de Nuits, Drouhin, Faiveley, Jadot, Rion, Rossignol
Best vintages	95, 94, 93, 92, 90, 89	95, 94, 93, 92	94, 93, 92

†: *has Grand Cru vineyards*

BOURGOGNE REGIONAL (Cont)	CÔTE DE NUITS	CÔTE DE NUITS (Cont)
Bourgogne Hautes Côtes de Beaune, Bourgogne Hautes Côtes de Nuits	Marsannay, Fixin (F), Gevrey-Chambertin†(GC), Morey St Denis†(MD), Chambolle-Musigny†(CM), Vougeot†(V)	Vosne-Romanée†(VR), Nuits-St-Georges (NtS), Côte de Nuits Villages (CN)
Bourgogne Hautes Côtes de Beaune: 993, Bourgogne Hautes Côtes de Nuits: 1,364	Marsannay: 398, Fixin: 237, Gevrey-Chambertin†: 1,220, Morey St Denis†: 319, Chambolle-Musigny†: 422, Vougeot†: 158	Vosne-Romanée: 554, Nuits-St-Georges: 741, Côte de Nuits Villages: 385
Total: 1.35 million	Total – Côte de Nuits: 2.04 million	n/a
Various: mainly limestone	Limestone and marls	Limestone and marls
(same)	Semi-Continental: cold winters but summers are often warm and dry.	(same)
Chardonnay, Pinot Noir	Pinot Noir, Chardonnay	Pinot Noir, Chardonnay
Similar to regional ACs but often with more intensity of fruit	Mainly reds. At their best these are some of the greatest and most seductive red wines in the world	Mainly reds. At their best these are some of the greatest and most seductive red wines in the world
Hautes Côtes de Nuits can be very good value.	Buy from a good producer or a respected merchant like Drouhin, Faiveley, Jadot, Louis Latour.	
2–5	5–25+	5–25+
	–**	**–****
Cave de Hautes Côtes de Beaune, Cave de Hautes Côtes de Nuits, Marcilly, Morot-Gaudry	F: Clair-Daü, Fougeray, Quillaret; F: Bordet, Rossignol; GC†: Bachelet, Burguet, Rousseau; MD: Clair, Dujac, Faiveley, Tardy; CM: Barthod-Noëllat, Roumier, de Vogüé; V†: Bertagna, Grivot, Leroy, Méo-Camuzet	VR: Arnoux, Engel, Lamarche, Méo-Camuzet, Mongeard-Mugneret, Domaine de la Romanée Conti, Nts: Faiveley, Dubois, Labouré-Roi, Michelot; CN: Durand, Rion, Rossignol
94, 93, 92	R: 92, 90, 89, 88, 85, 83, 78, 71	R: 92, 90, 89, 88, 85, 83, 78, 71

VINEYARD AREA:
70,500 acres

ANNUAL PRODUCTION:
634,014 gallons

CHAMPAGNE

Despite all the hype and disappointing bottles, the Champagne region still produces the greatest sparkling wine. The climate is chilly and is at the margins of grape growing. But this cool climate and chalky soil is ideal for bubbly. Here even more than other areas the name to follow is that of the producer not the appellation.

The bubbles are always created by secondary fermentation in bottle. Three grape varieties are used: one white (Chardonnay) and two black (Pinot Meunier and Pinot Noir). It is expensive to make good Champagne, so that with rare exceptions cheap Champagne and quality is a contradiction.

ABOVE *The Marne Valley where Pinot Meunier is the predominant grape.*

RECOMMENDED CHAMPAGNE HOUSES AND PRODUCERS

TOWNS	REIMS	EPERNEY	ELSEWHERE
Firm	Henriot, Charles Heidsieck, Krug Bruno Paillard, Palmer, Pol Roger, Pommery, Louis Roederer, Ruinart, Taittinger, Veuve Clicquot	Boizel, Charbaut, Charles de Casenove, Alfred Gratien, Moët & Chandon, Pol Roger	Bollinger, Deutz, Drappier, Gardet, Gosset, Jacquesson Laurent-Perrier Joseph Perrier, Philipponnat, Salon, Selosse, Vilmart

CHAMPAGNE AREAS
MAIN VINEYARD AREAS

Cool marginal climate with the more southerly Aube significantly warmer

AREA	MONTAGNE DE REIMS	CÔTE DES BLANCS	VALLÉE DE LA MARNE	AUBE
Size (acres)	18,950	13,593	19,600	16,062
Soils	Chalk and sand	Chalk	Chalk	Kimmeridgean clay
Grapes	Pinot Noir	Chardonnay	Pinot Meunier	Pinot Noir
Main villages	Ay, Bouzy, Chigny-les-Roses, Mareuil-sur-Ay, Sillery	Avize, Cramant, Mesnil-sur-Oger, Vertus, Vinay	Damery, Dizy, Hautvillers	Bar-sur-Aube, Bar-sur-Seine, Les Riceys

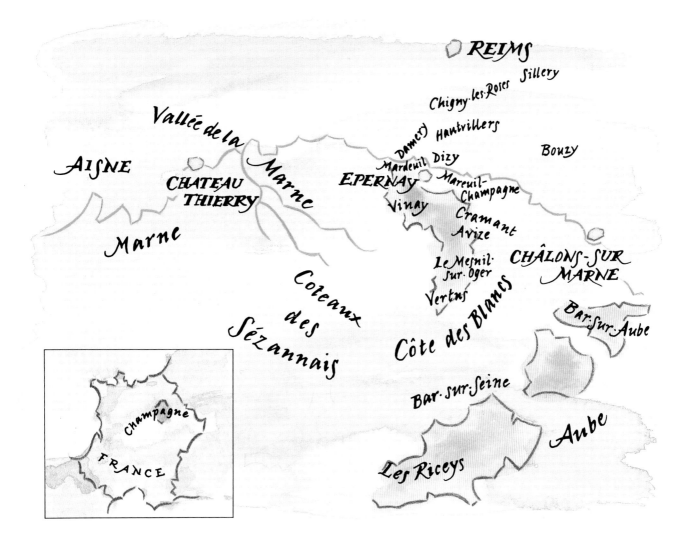

MY TEN FAVORITE
CHAMPAGNE HOUSES

FIRM	DATE FOUNDED	WHERE	OWNED BY	PRODUCTION (bottles)	RECOMMENDED CUVÉES
Billecart Salmon	1818	Mareuil-sur-Ay	Family owned	500,000	NV, 1985, 1988, Cuvée Nicolas François Billecart
Bollinger	1829	Ay	Family owned	1.5 million	NV, Grande Année 1985, 1988 R.D. 1982
Gardet	1890	Chigney-les-Roses	Family owned	600,000	NV, 1983
Gosset	1584	Ay	Max Cointreau	500,000	NV, Rosé, Grand Millésimé 1988
Alfred Gratien	1867	Epernay	Gratien et Meyer	150,000	NV, 1985
Krug	1843	Reims	Rémy Martin	500,000	Grande Cuvée, Rosé, 1982, 1985
Perrier Jouet	1811	Epernay	Seagrams	3 million	NV, 1985, 1988, Belle Epoque, 1985
Pol Roger	1849	Epernay	Family owned	1.4 million	NV, 1985, 1986, 1988, Cuvée Sir Winston Churchill, 85, 88
Louis Roederer	1776	Reims	Family owned	2 million	NV, 1985, 88, 89 Cristal, 1986, 88
Veuve Clicquot	1772	Reims	Louis Vuitton-Moët-Hennessy	10 million	NV, 85, 88, La Grande Dame, 85, 88

VINEYARD AREA:
36,200 acres

ANNUAL PRODUCTION:
422,676 gallons

ALSACE

This is the only French region to label its wines systematically by grape variety. It is also the only French region where Riesling is widely planted, producing Alsace's greatest wines.

The Vosges Mountains set the climate for Alsace. The vineyards lie in its rain shadow, making the region the driest areas of France after Roussillon. Winters can be cold but summer and autumn tend to be hot.

ABOVE *The medieval walls of Riquewihr—the most picturesque village in France's prettiest wine region.*

ALSACE

GRAPE VARIETY	GEWÜRZTRAMINER	MUSCAT	PINOT BLANC
Appellations	Alsace, Alsace Grand Cru, Vendange Tardive, Selection de Grains Nobles	Alsace, Alsace Grand Cru	Alsace, Crémant d'Alsace
Size (acres)	6,178	914	6,670
Style/taste	Very aromatic: spice, perfumed. The best show some restraint.	Always dry, aromatically orange and floral.	Lightly floral often more weight than versions from other countries.
Quality/buying tips	Because of its strong character tends to be a like or hate grape.	Well worth trying. Good quality but not one of Alsace's top wines.	Everyday drinking wine.
Aging potential	3–12	Best drunk young	Most best drunk young
Best producers	Beyer, Gassmann, Hugel, Willm	Dopff Irion, Gassmann, Trimbach	Blanck, Kreyden Weiss, Sipp, Turckheim
Price	**–***	*–**	*–**
Best vintages	93, 92, 90, 89, 88, 85	94, 93	94, 93

PINOT GRIS	PINOT NOIR	RIESLING	SYLVANER
Alsace, Alsace Grand Cru, Crémant d'Alsace, Vendange Tardive, Selection de Grains Nobles	Alsace, Crémant d'Alsace	Alsace, Alsace Grand Cru, Vendange Tardive, Selection de Grains Nobles	Alsace
2,174	2,470	7,413	5,807
Rich, round, and spicy.	Invariably pale, more like a rosé. Not Alsace's most successful variety.	Peaches, apple, steely acidity. "Gasoline" character develops with age.	Fresh, sometimes mineral or slightly floral.
Can be one of Alsace's finest wines.	With a few exceptions, rarely exciting.	Riesling makes many of the region's best wines.	Everyday drinking – less character than other grapes.
5–12	Most best drunk young	4–25	Best drunk young
Beyer, Hugel, Schleret, Schlumberger, Trimbach, Zind Humbrecht	Deiss, Hertz, Turckheim	Dopff au Moulin, Gisselbrecht, Hugel, Ostertag, Trimbach Zind Humbrecht	Rolly Gassmann Zind Humbrecht
–*	**–***	**–****	*–**
93, 92, 90, 89, 88, 86, 85, 83, 81, 76	92, 90, 89	92, 90, 89, 88, 85, 83	94, 93

BRITISH ISLES

Britain is at the northern limits of vine growing. Although vines were planted in Roman times and England produced a significant quantity of wine in the Middle Ages right up to the sixteenth century, winemaking finally petered out just before the First World War. Modern English and Welsh wine production dates from 1952, when the first new vineyard was planted. (Confusingly, so-called British Wine is made from imported grape juice and is *definitely not recommended*.)

Of the around 450 vineyards currently operating, most are in southern England: Kent, Sussex, Surrey, East Anglia and the far southwest. The most northerly vineyard is in south Yorkshire—there are no vineyards in Scotland. Denbies Estate in Dorking (Surrey), with 250 acres, is easily the largest. Other important vineyards include Lamberhurst, Thames Valley Vineyards, and Three Choirs.

Because of the marginal grape-growing climate, the bulk of the wines are white often using a mixture of German varieties (Müller Thurgau) and hybrids such as Seyval Blanc. Many of the vineyards are small and wines can vary greatly in quality, although standards have improved over the last ten years. The cool climate gives crisp fruit and the wines often need several years in bottle to show their best. However, a small amount of red and rosé is made. Also, an increasing amount of sparkling wine is being produced. As parts of England have a similar climate and soils to Champagne, some think that bubbles are the best hope for English wine.

Ireland has a few small vineyards on the east of the country.

RIGHT *Denbies Wine Estate—with 250 acres of vines, this is easily England's largest wine producer.*

GERMANY

⊕ VINEYARD AREA:
246,360 acres

🍾 ANNUAL PRODUCTION:
354 million gallons

🍷 ANNUAL CONSUMPTION
PER HEAD (GALLONS):
1973: 5.7 (West
Germany only)
1993: 6

HAMBURG

BERLIN

Rhein

BONN

Rheingau

FRANKFURT

Mosel-Saar
Ruwer

Nahe

Rheinhessen

Franken

LUXEMBOURG

Pfalz

STRASBOURG

Baden

Wurttemburg

MUNICH

AUSTRIA

FRANCE

Rhein

SWITZERLAND

ABOVE *Bernkastel and the Mosel from the famous Doktor vineyard.*

RIGHT *The best vineyards are sited on the steep, slate hillsides of Urzig in the Mosel Valley.*

Many parts of Germany are right at the limits of grape growing. Differences in microclimate, slope, and how long grapes are exposed to the sun are all important. Delicate, thrillingly flavorsome wines low in alcohol are a specialty of Germany. The best wines—from the Mosel, in particular—are unique. Riesling is also a specialty and most of Germany's top wines are made from this variety.

Sadly, the Germans make it difficult for the wine drinker because of their overcomplicated labeling. There is a huge difference between Bereich Bernkastel and a Bernkastel Doktor, the former being a cheap sugary concoction and the latter one of the country's greatest and most expensive wines. But unless the consumer is prepared to learn a long list of vineyard names, it is easy to be confused by which is which. The only thing to do is to remember the names of good producers. After all life is too short and there are too many interesting wines from elsewhere in the world to spend time peering at long unpronounceable names in arcane Gothic script. That is a shame because there have been a series of good vintages since 1988.

GERMANY

REGION	PFALZ	FRANKEN	WURTTEMBERG	BADEN
Climate	Hottest, driest German wine growing area. Similar to Alsace	Continental: cold winters, danger of spring frosts, warm summers	Continental	Warmer than many other areas
Size (acres)	58,620	15,063	27,510	40,586
Avg. Vol. (gal.)	53.55 million	14.38 million	29.11 million	30.58 million
Soils	Very varied	Varied: clay, limestone	Varied inc. chalk	Large area with very varied soils
Chief grapes	Müller Thurgau, Riesling, Kerner, Portugieser, Silvaner, Schreurebe	Müller Thurgau, Silvaner, Kerner	Riesling, Trollinger, Pinot Meunier, Kerner, Müller Thurgau, Lemberger	Müller Thurgau, Pinot Noir, Pinot Gris, Riesling, Pinot Blanc, Silvaner
Style	Wide range of styles, fresh dry whites often with intense flavors. Some reds from Pinot Noir and Dornfelder.	Mainly dry whites, often with a minerally tang. Small amounts of interesting Pinot Noir.	Mainly light, insipid reds from Trollinger and Lemberger. Some steely Rieslings.	Full, ripe fruit for both whites and reds. Quite French in style.
Quality/buying tips	Many high quality producers making some of Germany's most exciting wines.	Look out for Silvaners and for the traditional *Bocksbeutel* dumpy bottle.	A few quality producers, otherwise thin wines – curiosity value only.	Interesting wines from both co-ops and private growers.
Aging potential	6–25	3–15	Drink young	2–7
Price	*–***	**–***	**–***	*–***
Best producers	Bassermann-Jordan, Bürklin-Wolf, Von Buhl, Darting, Lingenfelder, Müller Catoir	Bürgerspital, Fürst, Juliusspital, Wirsching	Adelmann, Bauer, Neipperg	Bercher, Heger, Johner, Stigler; co-ops: Breisach, Burkheim, Durbach
Best vintages	93, 92, 90, 89, 88, 85, 83, 81, 76	93, 92, 90, 89, 88, 83, 76	—	93, 92, 89, 88

GERMANY

REGION	MOSEL-SAAR-RUWER	NAHE	RHEINGAU	RHEINHESSEN
Climate	Cold winters, warmish summers, especially on best protected slopes	Dry and a little warmer than Mosel	Sheltered position makes it warmer than Nahe and Rheinhessen	Close to the Rhine similar to Rheingau, cooler away from river
Size (acres)	31,431	11,488	8,169	64,407
Avg. Vol. (gal.)	31.42 million	10.64 million	4.61 million	63.46 million
Soils	Slate on best sites	Various: slate, loam, sandstone	Slate	Sandstone and slate/rich loam
Chief grapes	Riesling, Müller Thurgau, Kerner	Muller Thürgau, Riesling, Silvaner, Weissburgunder	Riesling	Muller Thürgau, Silvaner, Kerner, Scheurebe
Style	At best an amazingly delicate balance between crisp fruit and steely acidity.	Fuller more grapey wines than Mosel.	Often made in ultra-dry Trocken style. Otherwise some of Germany's richest and fullest Rieslings.	Mostly grapey and semi-sweet wines.
Quality/buying tips	Choose a Riesling from a top grower. Avoid Piesporter Michelsberg.	Some of Germany's Best Rieslings and often good value because Nahe is not well known.	Many of Germany's top estates are here. However, many find the Trocken style too lean to appeal.	Largely mass-produced cheap wine, e.g. Liebfraumilch. Has been a big export success.
Aging potential	10–50 depending upon sweetness	5–25+	7–50+	Drink young except for recommended producers
Price	*–****	**–***	**–****	*–***
Best producers	Grans-Fassian, Maximim Grunhaus, Haag, Loosen, J.J. Prum, Richter, Thanisch, Wegler-Deinhard; Saar: Hovel, Saarstein, Simon	A.E. Anheuser, Paul Anheuser, Crusius, Shafer	Breuer, Ress, Schloss Johannisberg, Weil	Gunderloch, Guntrun, Heyl Zu Herrnsheim
Best vintages	93, 92, 90, 89, 88, 85, 83, 76	94, 93, 92, 90, 89, 88, 85, 83, 76	93, 92, 90, 89, 88, 85, 83, 76	93, 92, 90, 89, 88, 85, 83, 763

AUSTRIA AND HUNGARY

VINEYARD AREA:
Austria: 143,300 acres
Hungary: 250,000 acres

**ANNUAL PRODUCTION
GALLONS:**
Austria: 68.4 million
Hungary: 102.5 million

**ANNUAL CONSUMPTION
PER HEAD (GALLONS):**
1973: 9.7 (Austria)
10.2 (Hungary)
1993: 9.1 (Austria)
8.4 (Hungary)

AUSTRIA

Deliciously fruity reds, crisp intense dry whites and remarkably varied and concentrated sweet wines, Austria has them all. Forget the old antifreeze scandal; ten years on this country is now producing some of Europe's most exciting wines. They often combine the fruit of the "New World" with the acidity and style of the Old. The presentation of many of the top wines is now clearly influenced by Italian chic with stylish bottles and labels. This is not surprising as some Austrian producers such as Alois Kracher and Willie Opitz are sophisticated and charismatic characters.

The one problem with Austrian wine is that, with the exception of many late harvest wines, it is expensive. As most of the wine is sold to the home market, there is little incentive for the Austrian producers to compete on the international market. This is a pity, for the quality of Austrian wine deserves to be better known.

All of the vineyards are in the eastern third of the country. The majority are clustered around Vienna. To the south of the city there is the area around Gumpoldskirchen and the vineyards around the shallow Neusiedlersee, whose microclimate provokes noble rot. Many of Austria's remarkable botrytis wines come from here. South of this lake are the vineyards of Burgenland, followed by the scattered Syrian vineyards

RIGHT *Sunset over the Neusiedlersee where the regular autumnal mists that rise from the lake practically guarantee "noble rot" every year. This permits a remarkable range of sweet wines to be made here.*

down on the Slovenian border. In the suburbs of Vienna there are vines, making this the only quality wine-producing capital city in the world. Northwest of Vienna, in the valley of the Danube, are the important regions of Krems and the Wachau. The Wachau is famous for the quality of its Rieslings.

The chief grape varieties are Grüner Veltliner, Müller-Thurgau, Muscat, Pinot Gris, Riesling, and Weissburgunder for the whites. Chardonnay and Sauvignon Blanc are increasingly planted. The leading red varieties are Blauburgunder (Pinot Noir), Blaufränkisch (native grape making very attractive wines packed with berry fruit, often best drunk young), St. Laurent (another native grape and possibly related to Pinot Noir), and Zweigelt (making lovely chunky cherry-flavored wines cut with zinging acidity). Most wine labels include the grape variety.

The Austrians use a quality system that is very similar to that of Germany. There are three categories of wine: Tafelwein, Landwein, and Qualitätswein. Additionally a wine may be labeled *Kabinett, Spätlese, Auslese, Eiswein, Beerenauslese, Ausbruch,* or *Trockenbeerenauslese,* depending on how sweet the grapes were when picked.

BEST PRODUCERS
KREMS: Lenz Moser, Josef Nigl, Winzer Krems
NEUSIEDLERSEE: Erich Henrich, Anton Kollwentz, Alois Kracher, Willie Opitz, Georg Steigelmar, Josef Umathum
STYRIA: Alois Gross, Sattler
VIENNA: Fuhrgassl-Huber, Franz Mayer, Herbert Schilling and Fritz Wieninger
WACHAU: Leo Alzinger, Franz Hirtzberger, Emmerich Knoll, Franz Pichler, Franz Prager
BEST RECENT VINTAGES: 93, 92, 91, 90, 88, 86, 85

BELOW *Vineyards in Hungary's Eger region.*

HUNGARY

Of all the former Iron Curtain countries Hungary has aroused the most interest. Much of the interest has been directed at one area at the far eastern end of the country: the Tokaji region.

In the seventeenth and eighteenth centuries Tokaji was the most famous sweet wine in the world. Now large companies from all over the world are investing in its renaissance. Investors include French insurance companies, Suntory of Japan, and Vega Sicilia from Spain. Furmint and Hárslevelü are the two principal varieties used and the Tokaji region is particularly prone to autumnal mists, so noble rot often develops here. The nobly rotted grapes are kept separate and then added to dry white wine that has already finished. The measures used are called *puttonyos* and the more *puttonyos* added the sweeter, finer, and more expensive the wine. Tokaji is labeled between 3 and 6 *puttonyos*. The Royal Tokaji Wine Company is the first of the new producers to release any Tokaji. Other bottles currently available were made under the Communist regime. The best recent Tokaji vintage was 1993.

Elsewhere there are a number of areas producing good-quality dry whites and reds at reasonable prices. The Eger region is famous for its Bull's Blood red, though sadly today's version must come from a very anemic bull. Farther west at Gyöngyös, good Chardonnay and Sauvignon Blanc are being produced. South of Budapest the large Balatonboglár winery makes a range of well-made, reasonably priced wines including some good rich Cabernet Sauvignon and some *cuvé close* sparkling wine.

ABOVE *Old mold-covered bottles in the cellars of the Tokaj Wine Trust at Toksva, Hungary. The trust has almost 200 cellars scattered around the Tokaj hills.*

BELOW *Vineyards at Tokaj.*

THE REST OF EASTERN EUROPE

 ANNUAL PRODUCTION:
51.9 million gallons
(1992)

 ANNUAL CONSUMPTION PER HEAD (GALLONS):
1973: 7.24
1993: 5.84

BELOW *Vineyards in the Khan Krum microregion, near Shumen, Bulgaria. The limestone soil here favors white varieties.*

E astern Europe has become the supplier of cheap wines to the rest of Europe. Throughout the region quality is decidedly variable but as these countries change from the Soviet system to private ownership there is an inevitably difficult transition. Most wines are sold under their varietal names. As well as international varieties look out for local ones like Kéfrankos and Saperavi.

BULGARIA

Good-quality but inexpensive Bulgarian Cabernet Sauvignon became an enormous success from the late 1970's. The Bulgarians successfully sold their wines using varietal labeling, also supplying good Merlot and some interesting blends of well-known varieties,

ABOVE *Vineyards above a village 2 miles west of Melnik in the south west corner of Bulgaria. Beyond are the sandstone cliffs of Melnik and the Pirin Mountains.*

such as Cabernet and Merlot, with lesser-known ones like Gamza and Cinsault. The native red varieties, Mavrud and Melnik, are also good, producing Bulgaria's most individual wines. White wines are much less successful. The Controliran quality system, similar to the French appellations, was introduced in 1985.

The 1985 Gorbachev anti-alcohol reforms and the uncertainties of privatization program that followed the fall of Communism have meant that some of the vineyards have not been looked after properly. Despite their export success, production in the Bulgarian vineyards has actually fallen since the late 1980's—nearly 80 million gallons were produced in 1990.

Although quality is now variable, the long-term future should be good, providing that sufficient investments are made.

Best producers include Melnik, Russes and Sliven. Unfortunately, the well-known Lovico Suhindol winery is uneven.

MOLDOVA

One of the newly independent countries following the breakup of the Soviet Union, Moldova lies between Romania and the Ukraine on the Black Sea. Although Moldova has the potential to produce interesting wines, unfortunately there has been little sign of this so far. Apart from some old aged reds, the wines to date have been bland and boring at best, despite the involvement of Penfolds of Australia.

 VINEYARD AREA:
444,780 acres

 ANNUAL PRODUCTION:
26.4 million gallons

VINEYARD AREA:
667,170 acres

ANNUAL PRODUCTION:
151.6 million gallons

ANNUAL CONSUMPTION PER HEAD (GALLONS):
1973: 9.4
1993: 5.0

ABOVE *Stanko Curin's vines at Kog, Eastern Slovenia.*

RIGHT *Slovenia: the steeply ridged hills just south of Lutomer—some of Slovenia's most picturesque vineyards are found here.*

VINEYARD AREA:
358,300 acres

ANNUAL PRODUCTION:
n/a

ANNUAL CONSUMPTION PER HEAD (GALLONS):
1973: 4.2
1993: 0.71

ROMANIA

Romania is the world's tenth largest producer. The vineyards are scattered in pockets throughout the country. Of the reds, Pinot Noir has been the most successful. Unfortunately quality, even from the same supplier can be very variable. The most interesting wines are sweet, in particular those made from the Tamaioasa grape in the Dealul Mare region.

SLOVENIA

The northern part of former Yugoslavia is beginning to show its potential. From its western vineyards come good reds and dry whites, made in a style akin to northern Italy. The go-ahead cooperative of Vipava is particularly good: the Merlot and Sauvignon Blanc are well worth trying. Wine from the eastern vineyards is more Germanic in style and is the origin of the bland Lutomer Riesling and made from Laski Riesling. However, private growers such as Stanko Curin in his steeply rolling vineyard in Kog are able to conjure up a fascinating range of flavors from this often despised grape. Curin even makes *eiswein*. Slovenia is definitely a country to watch.

RUSSIA, GEORGIA, AND UKRAINE

The Soviet Union used to be the fourth largest wine producer in the world. Since the breakup, many of the best vineyards lie outside Russia in Crimea and Georgia. There are a wide range of varieties planted in Russia but Rkatsiteli makes up half the plantings. Apart from the occasional bottle of *demi-sec* Champanski, very little Russian wine is seen outside the country. Georgia produces powerful tannic wines. From Massandra in Crimea (southern Ukraine) some exceptional fortified Muscats are made. In 1990 at Sotheby's in London there was an auction of old wines from the Czar's cellars.

LEBANON

VINEYARD AREA:
71,600 acres

ANNUAL PRODUCTION:
n/a

ANNUAL CONSUMPTION PER HEAD (GALLONS):
1973: n/a
1993: n/a

It is ironic that we should be surprised to find good wine in Lebanon. After all, wine was made here long before the birth of Christ. However, religious restrictions and the recent civil war has greatly reduced the amount of wine produced. Only about 10 percent of Lebanon's vineyards are used to produce wine, most of the production is used as table grapes or for raisins.

Most of Lebanon's vineyards are in the cooler Bekaa Valley with the vines planted at high altitudes. The Hochar's Château Musar is the best-known estate. Despite having vineyards separated from the winery by the front line, Serge Hochar managed remarkably to make wine throughout the civil war except in 1976 and 1984. In 1984 the grapes were held up and had rotted by the time they were released. These spicy, ripe wines are made from Cabernet Sauvignon, Cinsault, and Syrah and they age well.

With the ending of the civil war, other estates, such as Domaine de Kefraya (620 acres) are emerging. The best wine is Château de Kefraya, which is made from Cabernet Sauvignon, Grenache and Cinsault. Like Musar, this wine needs to age.

RIGHT *The view from Kefraya to the western side of the Bekaa Valley. Most vineyards are found on the western side.*

CHINA AND INDIA

 VINEYARD AREA (CHINA):
161,000 acres

 Unfortunately there are no reliable figures for wine production and consumption in China.

For the moment most people's experience of Chinese wines is ordering a bottle out of curiosity in a Chinese restaurant. Chinese wines found on the international market come from joint ventures with western liquor companies. Best known are the Beijing Friendship Winery (Pernod-Ricard); Hua Dong, which produces, with Australian help, Chardonnay and Riesling under the Tsingtao label; and Rémy Martin's Dynasty.

As China becomes more open to the world and its economy expands, its wine industry is likely to expand too. For instance, the large Plaimont Cooperative in southwestern France has recently signed an agreement to produce wine and Seagrams also has a joint venture. However, the Chinese have a strong tradition of drinking liquor.

India has a very small wine production. Although there are 125,000 acres of vines planted, only a tiny proportion is used to make wine. The bottle fermented sparkling wine, Omar Khayyam, is easily the best known. Made near Poona, south east of Bombay, it is in the medium price range and is worth trying.

ABOVE *The Hua Dong winery, Qingdao province, China.*

RIGHT *Champagne India Ltd where Omar Khayyam is made.*

SOUTH AFRICA

⊕	**VINEYARD AREA:** 251,200 acres
🍾	**ANNUAL PRODUCTION:** 124.2 million gallons
🍷	**ANNUAL WINE CONSUMPTION PER HEAD (GALLONS):** 1973: 2.8 1993: 2.4

South Africa's vineyards are confined to a relatively thin coastal strip. They run from Vredendal in the Northwest, past Cape Town and eastward into the Klein Karoo. Only the vineyards of the Orange River, the country's hottest grape growing area, lie outside this area.

Everyone agrees that South African wines have a terrific potential and now, with the coming of democracy in 1994, they have the chance to show how good they can be. But it will take a little while to reveal their full potential because during the apartheid years the South Africans fell behind the Australians and Californians.

This is partly because with South Africa cut off from the rest of the world, the exchange of ideas and knowledge with other winemakers was limited. Neither did the world market have an influence on the wines being made. Also, South Africa operated a quarantine policy for importing vines and until recently it was very difficult to import top-quality vines into the country. The result is that many of South Africa's vines are either low quality or are seriously diseased. This is now being put right but it will take time.

SOUTH AFRICA

REGION	COASTAL REGION	BREEDE RIVER VALLEY
Areas: Wine of Origin zones (WO)	Constantia, Paarl, Stellenbosch, Swartland, Tulbagh	Robertson, Worcester
Climate	Mediterranean style	Drier, hotter so irrigation required
Chief grapes	Chardonnay, Riesling, Sémillon; Cabernet Sauvignon, Cabernet Franc, Pinotage, Shiraz	Chardonnay, Colombard, Riesling, Sauvignon Blanc; Shiraz
Size (acres)	118,877	73,883
Avg. Vol. (gal.)	79.81 million	99.24 million
Style	Constantia: mainly whites Stellenbosch: mainly red	Robertson: mostly whites
Quality/buying tips	Stellenbosch: some of SA's best reds.	Robertson: good Chardonnay and also Shiraz.
Price	*–***	*–***
Best producers	Avontuur, Boschendal, Fairview, Glen Carlou, Kanonkop, Nederberg (Cabernet & late harvest), Rosenview, Simonsig, Simonsvlei, Swartland Co-op, Thelema, Twee Jonge Gezellen, Villiera Estate, Vriesenhof, Warwick Estate, Zonnebloem	Beck, Bon Courage, De Wetshof, Van Louveren Weltevrede

KLEIN KAROO	OLIFANTS RIVER	OVERBERG DISTRICT
As above	As above	Elgin, Walker Bay
Hot and dry, cool winters. Irrigation required	Hot summers, low rainfall but heat moderated by Atlantic	Mediterranean but proximity to Atlantic gives cool climate
Chenin Blanc, Muscadel	Chardonnay, Chenin Blanc, Colombard, Muscadel; Cabernet Franc, Cabernet Sauvignon, Cinsault	Chardonnay, Pinot Noir, (Sauvignon Blanc)
8,152	19,770	n/a
10.43 million	26 million	n/a
Wide range of white and rosé. Dessert and fortified wines from Muscadel.	Mainly cheap, bland wines from high yields.	More restrained, elegant cool climate style with intensity of flavor for reds and whites.
Dessert and fortified wines can be bargains and are well worth trying.	Good value reds and whites from Vredendal Co-op.	Small high quality production. Some of SA's best wines from this promising area.
*–**	*–**	**–***
Boplaas, Die Krans	Spruitdrift Co-op, Vredendal Co-operative	Bouchard Finlayson, Hamilton Russell, Vergelegen

ABOVE *Dieu Donne Estate in the Franschoek Valley, Cape Province, South Africa.*

Chenin Blanc is still the most planted grape. In South Africa it is called Steen and is used to make a wide range of styles from dry through to "sherry" styles. Because of high yields and because it is rarely planted on the best sites, South African Chenin is rarely more than inoffensively bland. However, the occasional late harvest wines, such as those from Zonnebloem, show what might be made.

Really, the future of South Africa lies with other international grape varieties such as Chardonnay, Riesling, and Sauvignon Blanc—for white wines—and Cabernet Sauvignon, Pinot Noir, and Shiraz for reds. There have also been some good results with Cabernet Franc, especially from Norma Ratcliffe's Warwick Estate. One should not forget Pinotage, the country's true specialty. This is a cross between Pinot Noir and Cinsault and was created in 1926. Previously known as a rustic, jammy wine with all the subtlety of an elephant, some producers such as Kanonkop and Warwick Estate are now making impressively individual Pinotages.

There are 13 Wines of Origin Zones. This system is similar to France's AC and Spain's DO systems and was introduced in 1972.

Some 90 percent of South African wine is still made by 70 co-operatives and these are very variable in quality. However, the best of these cooperatives are providing well-made wine at a bargain price for the export market, whereas the small number of private estates are concentrating on the upper price range and raising South Africa's profile. Most of the private estates are in the Coastal Region especially in the Stellenbosch WO. But quality wine is now being made in other areas, where individual winemakers show the way.

One of the pioneers was Tim Hamilton Russell, who in the 1970s planted Chardonnay and Pinot Noir at Hemel-en-Aarade Valley near Hermanos, south of Cape Town. The moderating influence of the Atlantic Ocean gives a cool climate. The first vintage was 1981.

RIGHT *Laborie Estate, Paarl, with the Paarl Rock in the distance, Cape Province, South Africa.*

Although the Hamilton Russell Pinot Noirs have had most press attention, the Chardonnay is very good and probably less variable.

Another pioneer has been Danie de Wet. At the De Wetshof Estate (now covering 350 acres) he has shown that Chardonnay can be successfully grown in South Africa and that quality wines can be made in the Robertson area. Although Danie is large and ruggedly built, his Chardonnays are attractively restrained. He is careful not to overdo the use of new oak and so avoids the dreary wood dust and vanilla essence aromas and flavors of too many wines where oak has been crudely used.

The best South African wines have Australian fruit style allied to the acidity and style of European ones. It seems certain that South African wines will develop enormously over the next ten years.

AUSTRALIA

VINEYARD AREA:
148,260 acres

ANNUAL PRODUCTION:
121.5 million gallons

ANNUAL CONSUMPTION PER HEAD (GALLONS):
1973: 2.9
1993: 4.1

B ig, blackcurranty Cabernet Sauvignons, Chardonnays full of tropical fruit and laced with toasty vanilla flavors, and concentrated spicy Shiraz have established Australia as a good-value, quality wine producer. Its wines have turned on a new generation of drinkers to wine. The emphasis on fruit has changed ideas in Europe, especially in France where the Aussie threat has sometimes been viewed with consternation and panic.

The effect of the Australian approach can now be seen in the classic areas of France where the lessons learnt down under have been applied. Red Bordeaux made since the late 1980's has noticeably more emphasis on fruit and is ready to drink much sooner than it traditionally was. "Will it last as long as it used to?" is the question many ask. As yet nobody knows.

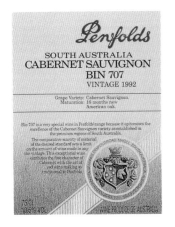

RIGHT *Stormy light in early morning over Mountadam Estate vineyards, 656 yards up on the High Eden Ridge in the South Mount Lofty Ranges, southern Australia.*

Grapes may be transported hundreds of miles from vineyard to winery, so the link here between the land and the wine is much less important than it is in France. This is especially true for the lower- and medium-priced Australian wines. However, top Australian wines, such as Penfolds Magill Estate and Henschke's Hill of Grace tend to be much more specific about from where the grapes have been sourced. Growers like Brian Croser of Petaluma and Adam Wynn of Mountadam have always thought that where vines are planted is very important.

It is just that Australians have not been hidebound by long tradition like the French and Germans, so they have been able to experiment and try out new ideas. New vine trellising systems are being used to increase the amount of leaf cover and, thus, photosynthesis all to maximize fruit ripening. Experiments to see whether it is really necessary to spend four months during the winter pruning are going on. Now in some vineyards there is no or minimal pruning.

It is this willingness to experiment and the refusal to accept without challenge the traditional ways of vine growing and wine-making that has helped to make Australia currently the most successful wine-producing country. The differences between the traditional vineyards of France and those of Australia are marked.

Although there are many fine small wineries, a few big companies dominate Australian winemaking. Fortunately these firms produce consistent quality and their top wines are among Australia's best. Penfolds is easily the largest. Within this corporation are the Lindemans, Seppelt, and Wynns brands. Penfolds, or Southcorp

RIGHT *New vineyards on the eastern slopes of the Barossa Range, near Pewsey Vale, in South Africa.*

BOTTOM RIGHT *Moving sheep by "Hill of Grace" vineyard of Henschke, where the Shiraz vines are over 100 years old.*

Wines, has a big range of wines from good-value Koonunga Hill (a Cabernet Shiraz blend) and Lindemans Bin 65 Chardonnay (the archetypal Aussie powerful, buttery oaky Chardonnay) up to Bin 707 Cabernet Sauvignon and finally Grange, made from Shiraz. BRL Hardy is Australia's second firm and includes Houghton and Château Reynella.

There have always been strong characters in the Australian wine industry. It was Max Schubert of Penfolds who created Grange Hermitage, now agreed to be the greatest wine made in the Southern Hemisphere. Schubert first made Grange in 1951 after a visit to

Tiers vineyard of Petaluma viewed over Pfitzner vineyard, Piccadilly Valley, Adelaide Hills.

PETALUMA

1993 CHARDONNAY
PICCADILLY VALLEY

750 ml
13.5% Vol

PRODUCE OF AUSTRALIA BOTTLED AT PICCADILLY SA

Europe to study sherry-making in Jerez. At this time fortified wines were the completely dominant style in Australia. On his way home Schubert passed through Bordeaux, where he discovered the use of French oak in making great red Bordeaux. On his return to Australia and determined to emulate the great Bordeaux wines, Schubert was forced to improvize with Shiraz and American oak because there wasn't any Cabernet Sauvignon or French oak available. After initial derision because these wines were so different from the Australian norm, the quality of Grange has been recognized as well as the contribution of Schubert to modern Australian wine.

Brian Croser, at Petaluma, is one of the most conspicuous of the country's winemakers, managing to harness power with delicacy. He makes fine Cabernet Sauvignon and Riesling, and one of Australia's best Chardonnays. His sparkling wine, modestly called Croser, is made in partnership with Bollinger and is one example of a number of increasingly fine sparkling wines now being made here.

Australia is beginning to suffer from its success. The last three vintages have been short and this, coupled with the international popularity of Australian wines means that there is now a lack of wine and that prices are beginning to go up. However, the Australians are busy planting new vineyards. As well as trying to satisfy world demand, there is also a search for sites in cooler climate areas, away from the blasting heat which ripens the grapes but does not give very interesting flavors.

A USTRALIA

REGION	NEW SOUTH WALES	VICTORIA
Climate	Hot and dry. Irrigation vital in many areas.	Big range from the heat of the Murray River to the cool Yarra Valley.
Size (acres)	27,428	48,251
Avg. Vol. (gal.)	44.91 million	19.81 million
Chief vineyard areas	Hunter Valley, Mudgee, Murrumbigee	Bendigo, Geelong, Gippsland, Goulburn, Grampians, Pyrenees, Yarra Valley
Chief grape varieties	Chardonnay, Sémillon, Trebbian; Cabernet Sauvignon, Shiraz	Chardonnay, Muscadelle, Muscat; Cabernet Sauvignon, Pinot Noir, Shiraz
Style	Tropical fruit Chardonnays. Rich, concentrated Shiraz.	Huge range but some very powerful Shiraz.
Quality/buying tips	Old Sémillons are a revelation.	Large quantities of jug wine but also some very high quality estates.
Price	*–***	*–***
Best producers	De Bortoli, Botobolar, Lark Hill, Lake's Folly, Lindemans, Rosemount, Rothbury Estate, Tyrrells	Bannockburn, Brown Brothers, Chateau Tahbilk, Coldstream Hills, Hanging Rock Winery, Kings Creek, Langi Ghiran, Michelton, Taltarni, Virgin Hills, Yarra Yering, Yeringberg
Best vintages	91, 90, 87, 86	94, 93, 92, 91, 90, 88

TASMANIA	SOUTH AUSTRALIA	WESTERN AUSTRALIA
Cool climate in comparison to the rest of Australia. Short of water in some areas.	Potentially very warm climate moderated by the sea's cooling influence. Some cool climate areas.	Big climatic variations. Very hot in Swan Valley to cool in Mount Barker-Frankland region. Drought is frequently a problem.
717	57,500	4,942
n/a	58.12 million	1.32 million
Coal River, Derwent Valley, Pipers Brook, Tamar Valley	Adelaide Hills (A), Barossa (B), Clare Valley (Cl), Coonawarra (Co), Eden Valley (E), McLaren Vale (Mc), Murray Malee, Padthaway	Margaret River, Mount Barker-Frankland, Warren-Blackwood
Chardonnay, Riesling; Cabernet Sauvignon, Pinot Noir	Chardonnay, Riesling, Sauvignon Blanc, Sémillon; Cabernet Sauvignon, Shiraz	Chardonnay, Chenin Blanc, Sémillon, Verdelho; Cabernet Sauvignon, Grenache, Merlot
Often vibrant fruit with good acidity.	Big variation between elegantly restrained wines to powerful oaky reds and whites.	At their best intense flavored whites and powerful reds.
Pinot Noir, Chardonnay and Rieslings can be excellent. Look for the high-quality sparkling wines.	All of Australia's major firms are here. Huge range of qualities.	Increasingly good wines coming from the cooler climate areas.
—*	*—****	*—***
Heemskerk, Moorilla Estate, Pipers Brook	A: Basedow, Petaluma; B: Leo Buring, Peter Lehmann, Charles Melton, Penfolds, St Hallett, Yalumba; Cl: Knappstein; Co: Hollick, Katnook, Lindemans, Parker Estate, Penley Estate, Rouge Homme, Wynns Coonawarra; E: Heggies, Henschke, Hill-Smith, Mountadam; Mc: BRL Hardy, Geoff Merrill, Mount Hurtle	Cape Mentelle, Evans & Tate, Houghton includes Moondah Brook, Leeuwin, Plantagent, Vasse Felix
91, 90, 86, 85	93, 91, 90, 88	94, 92, 91, 90, 89

NEW ZEALAND

ABOVE *Machine harvesting in Montana's Brancott Estate vineyards, Marlborough.*

O f all of the new producing countries to have emerged onto the world stage, New Zealand has had the most astonishing progress. Until the mid-1970's New Zealand produced uninteresting Germanic style wines for the home market. Then they started planting the familiar international varieties such as Chardonnay, Sauvignon Blanc, Cabernet Sauvignon, and Merlot. Now, with its Sauvignon Blanc in particular, New Zealand is producing wines that are world class within their style. The classic examples of cool-climate Sauvignon Blanc used to be Sancerre and Pouilly Fumé from the central vineyards of the Loire. Now, for many people, it is New Zealand Sauvignon Blanc, especially that from the Marlborough region at the northern end of South Island. Cloudy Bay, the epitome of New Zealand Sauvignon Blanc, is sold on allocation and is far harder to buy than any top-quality Loire Sauvignon.

As far as exports are concerned, there are no cheap New Zealand wines. They have the highest average bottle price of all the wine-producing countries of the world.

New Zealand has the coolest climate and the longest ripening season of all the Southern Hemisphere vineyards. The country's cool climate and its winemakers' skills has given it a winning combination of ripe fruit and crisp acidity for its whites.

As well as Sauvignon Blanc, increasingly good Chardonnays are being made. They have an appealing intensity and fullness of fruit.

RIGHT *Vineyard and winery of Nobilo Vintners, Huapai, near Auckland.*

VINEYARD AREA:
16,500 acres

ANNUAL PRODUCTION:
1.72 million gallons

ANNUAL CONSUMPTION PER HEAD (GALLONS):
1973: 2.3
1993: 4.4

The best Chardonnays are fermented and aged in new oak barrels and the wines have the structure to carry the oak. Inevitably some producers allow the oak to dominate. This tendency is made worse by most consumers' belief that Southern Hemisphere wines are ready to drink immediately. Often with a bit more bottle age the oak would soften down and marry with the wine. Although less fashionable, some excellent Rieslings and a few good Chenin Blancs are made. Given how unfashionable Chenin Blanc is, it is nor surprising that very few producers treat Chenin Blanc seriously. However, Millton and Collards have shown that New Zealand is capable of making the best Chenin Blanc outside its home in the Loire Valley.

Red wines have been less convincing. The Cabernet Sauvignons are often rather stalky and tannic, leaving a mean impression in the mouth. It is surprising that the earlier-ripening Cabernet Franc has not been more widely planted for it would seem better adapted to New Zealand's cooler climate areas such as Wairarapa and Marlborough than its more fashionable cousin. It may be that

RIGHT *Mission Vineyards and the seminary of the "Brothers of the Society of Mary" at Taradale, near Napier. Hawke Bay can be seen in the distance.*

Cabernet reds will improve as New Zealand winemakers become more experienced in making these wines and the vines become older. Pinot Noir, in contrast, has been much more successful and there are some delicious examples around.

Because of the world demand new vineyards are being planted and the area under vines is increasing by about 10 percent a year. At present the total plantings are about half the size of France's Muscadet appellations. But there remains a large potential area that would be suitable for growing vines. Already newly planted vineyards will soon increase the area in production to over 20,000 acres. If sales continue at their current rate, the New Zealand vineyard is likely to be substantially bigger in ten years' time than it is now.

RIGHT *Pinot Noir vines, Central Otago vineyard, Gibbston Valley.*

NEW ZEALAND
NORTH ISLAND

AREA	AUCKLAND/ WAIKATO	GISBORNE (POVERTY BAY)	HAWKES BAY	WAIRARAPA/ MARTINBOROUGH
Climate	Humid with rain in the fall.	Cooler and less sunny than Hawkes Bay.	Sunny, little fall rain. Danger of spring frosts.	Cool, often drought in summer. Windy.
Size (acres)	1,006	3,526	4,057 (5,604)*	464
Avg. Vol. (gal.)	n/a	n/a	n/a	n/a
Soils	Clay/sandy loam	Alluvial loam	Loam	Gravel, loam
Chief grape varieties	Chardonnay, Cabernet Sauvignon, Merlot	Chardonnay, Gewürztraminer, Müller Thurgau, Muscat, Sauvignon Blanc, Sémillon	Chardonnay, Chenin Blanc, Müller Thurgau, Sauvignon Blanc, Cabernet Sauvignon	Chardonnay, Cabernet Sauvignon, Pinot Noir
Style	Some full bodied Cabernet, rich Chardonnay.	Whites best: spicy opulent Gewürztraminer, some rich Chardonnays.	Wide range of styles. Sauvignon Blanc tends to be rounder and softer than from Marlborough.	Fruity, deep colored Pinot Noir, rich complex Chardonnay. Cabernet Sauvignon is often light.
Quality/buying tips	Almost more wineries here than vineyards. Many grapes are brought in.	Good Chenin Blanc, Gewürztraminer, Riesling.	Most consistent area for reds + some fine Chardonnay.	Small high quality production: good Chardonnay and Pinot Noir.
Price	**—***	**—***	**—***	**—***
Best producers	Babich, Collards, Coopers Creek, Corbans, Delegats, Kumeu River, Matua, Montana, Nobilo, Selak, Villa Maria	Millton, Corbaus	Esk Valley, Morton Estate, Ngatarawa, C.J. Pask, Te Mata, Vidal	Ata Rangi, Martinborough, Palliser Estate
Best vintages	94, 93, 91, 90	94, 93, 91, 89	94, 93, 91, 89	94, 93, 91, 90

NEW ZEALAND
SOUTH ISLAND

AREA	NELSON	MARLBOROUGH	CANTERBURY-CHRISTCHURCH	OTAGO
Climate	Warmest part of island but suffers from fall rains.	Coolish but with sunny days in summer.	Cool, dry but long sunny falls. Danger of spring frosts.	Center of island has a Continental climate. Short growing season but warm summer.
Size (acres)	227	5,177 (7,413)	514 (642)	119 (586)
Avg. Vol. (gal.)	n/a	n/a	n/a	n/a
Soils	Varied	Silt, gravel	Varied: silt, gravel, limestone	Varied inc. schist, silt
Chief grape varieties	Chardonnay, Gewürztraminer	Chardonnay, Riesling, Sauvignon, Blanc	Chardonnay, Riesling; Pinot Noir	Chardonnay, Gewürztraminer; Pinot Noir
Style	Elegant Chardonnay, lemon and lime Riesling.	Asparagus crisp Sauvignon, complex Chardonnays, botrytised Riesling.	Raspberry, plum Pinot Noir, some rich, tangy Chardonnays and steely Rieslings.	Really too early to say but there is crisp fruit and zingy acidity in some of the wines.
Quality/buying tips	Small but quality production.	Whites best especially new classic Sauvignon Blanc.	Big vintage variations.	Believed to have great potential.
Price	**–***	**–***	**–***	**–***
Best producers	Neudorf, Siefried	Cloudy Bay, Hunters, Montana, Vavasour, Wairau River	Giesen, St Helena, Waipara Springs	Chard Farm, Gibbston Valley, Rippon
Best vintages	94, 93, 92, 91	94, 93, 92, 91	94, 93, 92, 91	91, 92

† *Figures in parentheses include vineyards planted but not yet in production. Only figures for those regions which have substantial new plantings are given.*

CHILE

 VINEYARD AREA:
16,600 acres

 ANNUAL PRODUCTION:
83.5 million gallons

ANNUAL CONSUMPTION PER HEAD (GALLONS):
1973: 14.1
1993: 7.0

FAR RIGHT *A vine that is at least 100 years old at the Moures Estate, Chile.*

BELOW *The same estate, but these vines are just one year old.*

T he perfect climate for growing grapes and "ungrafted vines" have often been cited in the country's favor, leading to a prediction that "This will be Chile's year!" The problem is that this prognosis has been made every year since the beginning of this decade but somehow Chile has yet to really fulfill its promise.

Because of distance, the Atacama Desert, and the Andes, Chile is free from Phylloxera and so has been able to retain the ungrafted vines. These were imported into the country from Europe during the last century before the louse's devastating arrival in Europe. The climate in the grape-growing areas is well suited to growing disease-free grapes. There is little rain during the summer but summer temperatures are moderated by the cold Humboldt current that flows northward along the coast.

The vineyards are planted in the Central Valley. Until recently plantings have been concentrated in the Maipo Valley close to the capital Santiago and some 120 miles farther south around Curicó. Another area is the Aconcagua Valley, which is 50 miles north of Santiago and specializes in growing Cabernet Sauvignon.

Now new cool areas such as Casablanca, west of Santiago and cooled by fogs and winds off the Pacific Ocean, and the coastal region of Cauquenes, some 200 miles south of Valparaiso, are being developed for white varieties. Already impressively subtle Chardonnays are emerging from Casablanca.

ABOVE *Vineyards near Perdillo, Central Chile.*

The Pais is the most planted grape but this is for local consumption. Cabernet Sauvignon is the most widely planted premium red grape, followed by Merlot. Sauvignon, Sémillon, and Chardonnay make up the premium whites with the emphasis very much on Chardonnay. Chile is just starting to diversify away from the "International Quartet" of Chardonnay, Sauvignon Blanc, Cabernet Sauvignon, and Merlot. Bottles of Zinfandel and other varieties are beginning to appear.

Although the Chilean wine industry is dominated by large companies, several high-quality "boutique" wineries have recently started to emerge. A number of foreign companies and winemakers have been attracted to Chile. These include the Rothschilds of Château Lafite at Los Vascos, Denis Duveau and Henry Marionnet from the Loire Valley, as well as Torres at Lontué.

Leading producers include Caliterra, José Canepa, Concha y Toro, Cousiño Macul, Errázuriz, Montes, Santa Carolina, San Pedro, Santa Rita, Undurraga, and Los Vascos.

Undoubtedly Chilean wines have improved greatly over the past seven years. The reds that used to be aged in old wood for too long, giving them strangely stewed wood flavors, are being replaced by wines with fresh chunky fruit. Also Sauvignon Blancs, which were often disappointing, are improving. Many vines that were thought to be Sauvignon Blanc vines turned out to be another and less good kind of Sauvignon. These have been replaced.

Chile seems certain to remain a source of good-quality, medium-priced wine, but is also likely to provide some really top-quality bottles. The only question is: how long do we have to wait?

ARGENTINA, BRAZIL, MEXICO, AND URUGUAY

 VINEYARD AREA:
494,200 acres

 ANNUAL PRODUCTION:
380 million gallons

 ANNUAL CONSUMPTION PER HEAD (GALLONS):
1973: 19.0
1993: 12.6

ARGENTINA

Argentina appears to be the only South American country that will provide a real challenge to Chile in the quality wine stakes. It is by far the largest vineyard producer in South America, having three times as many acres of vines as Chile and is the world's sixth largest wine producer.

The vineyards run from Salta province in the north, close to the border with Paraguay and Bolivia, down to the Río Negro province, over a thousand miles south. The principal wine regions are the Río Grande (especially for sparkling wine), San Juan, and, in particular, Mendoza, where nearly three quarters of Argentina's vines are planted. The Mendoza vineyards are in the lee of the Andes with a hot and dry climate. Irrigation is essential. But the nighttime temperatures are low, allowing the grapes to develop flavor.

The use of more unusual grape varieties is one advantage that Argentina has. Some of Argentina's best reds are made from Malbec. Malbec produces deep, colored, tannic reds tasting of plum and other black fruits. Malbec is the principal variety of Cahors in the southwest of France where it is called Auxerrois. Torrontes and Sémillon are the most planted white varieties. The use of modern winemaking techniques are

RIGHT *View of the vineyards with Andes in the background at the Trapiche Estate, Mendoza.*

RIGHT *Catena's vineyards, one of Argentina's most promising producers, with the Pre-Cordillerra in the background.*

now producing fresher and more interesting whites. In contrast to this variety Chilean wines have been largely limited to the "International Quartet."

The largest company is Peñaflor, one of the largest wine firms in the world. Most of its production is cheap bulk wine but its boutique label, Trapiche, has done much to raise the international profile of Argentina. Its Malbec is particularly good as are the Reserve Cabernet Sauvignon and Chardonnay. Several other firms are now emerging such as Catena, a promising modern winery in Mendoza, San Telmo, Etchart, partly owned by Pernod-Ricard and based in Salta, and Bodegas Canale, in the Río Negro and making good whites. Bodegas Weinart in Mendoza makes old fashioned reds.

RIGHT *Barrels at the Trapiche Estate.*

VINEYARD AREA:
148,300 acres

 ANNUAL PRODUCTION:
97 million gallons

 ANNUAL CONSUMPTION PER HEAD (GALLONS):
1973: 0.52
1993: 0.48

BRAZIL

The bulk of the vineyards are in the south of the country. Because of the wet and humid climate, most of the vines are trained up high on pergolas. This is to help the grapes to dry out and reduce rot. Many of these vineyards are planted with *labrusca* or hybrid varieties. (*Labrusca* is botanical name for native American vine. These varieties tend to make wines of a markedly "foxy" flavor. *Vinefera* varieties have proved to be more popular.) Premium varieties make up considerably less than 20 percent of the area planted. Premium varieties planted include Barbera, Chardonnay, Cabernet Franc, Cabernet Sauvignon, Merlot, Muscat, Sémillon, and Trebbiano.

 VINEYARD AREA:
177,900 acres

 ANNUAL PRODUCTION:
n/a

 ANNUAL CONSUMPTION PER HEAD (GALLONS):
1973: n/a
1993: n/a

MEXICO

Vines were first planted by the Spaniards led by Cortes in the early sixteenth century. Mexico is now the fourth largest wine producer in Central and South America. However, most of the wine produced goes to make brandy and vermouth. Companies like Allied Domecq, Gonzalez Byass, Hennessy, and Martell are all involved in making brandy here. However over the last fifteen years there has been a greater accent on wine and some very drinkable and good value Cabernet Sauvignon has appeared on overseas shelves.

 VINEYARD AREA:
32,100 acres

 ANNUAL PRODUCTION:
21.1 million gallons

 ANNUAL CONSUMPTION PER HEAD (GALLONS):
1973: 6.7
1993: 7.0

URUGUAY

This is the fourth largest wine producer in South America. Production has increased by over a third since the 1970's. As yet little is exported but the Uruguayans now have a wine promotion body and their wines are beginning to be seen on the shelves of European supermarkets. The main premium grape varieties are Cabernet Sauvignon, Merlot, Pinot Noir, Tannat, as well as Gewürztraminer, Riesling, and Sémillon. However, over half the country's vines are hybrids.

BOOKS ON WINE

BURTON ANDERSON *Wine Atlas of Italy* (Mitchell Beazley, 1990). Burton Anderson is your best guide to Italian wine.

MICHAEL BROADBENT *Wine Tasting* (Mitchell Beazley, 1982). The classic guide to how to taste wine. Latest revised edition appeared in 1995.

OZ CLARKE *New Classic Wines* (Mitchell Beazley, 1991). Fresh approach and very readable account of the way the wine world has changed, with particular emphasis on "New World" producers.

MICHAEL COOPER *The Wines of Vineyards of New Zealand* (Hodder & Stoughton, 1993). Lively, detailed, and well-illustrated guide.

HUBRECHT DUIJKER *The Wine Atlas of Spain* (Mitchell Beazley, 1992). The latest book in English on the fast-changing wines of Spain.

MICHAEL EDWARDS *The Champagne Companion* (Apple Press 1994). Easy-to-use guide to champagne.

NICHOLAS FAITH *The Story of Champagne* (Hamish Hamilton, 1988). Detailed look at the history of Champagne that debunks the myth that Dom Pérignon was the inventor of sparkling wines.

Guide Hachette des Vins This is the best of the annual French wine guides.

JAMES HALLIDAY *Wine Atlas of Australia and New Zealand* (Harper Collins, 1991). Detailed and well-illustrated guide to the Antipodean wines that have revolutionized wine drinking.

JAMES HALLIDAY *Wine Atlas of California* (Harper Collins, 1993). Comprehensive survey of Californian wines and full of forthright good sense.

JAMES HALLIDAY AND HUGH JOHNSON *The Art and Science of Wine* (Mitchell Beazley, 1992). Explains winemaking in relatively everyday language.

ANTHONY HANSON *Burgundy* (Faber & Faber, 1995). The long-awaited 2nd Edition (1995) has just been published and is excellent.

HUGH JOHNSON *World Atlas of Wine* (Mitchell Beazley, 1994). Fascinating book that relates wine to the place where the grapes are grown.

HUGH JOHNSON *The Story of Wine* (Mitchell Beazley, 1989). Superb overview of the history of wine and how it has developed.

HUGH JOHNSON *Pocket Wine Book* (Mitchell Beazley). Despite increased competition, this is still the best annual wine guide.

FRANK JONES *The Save Your Heart Wine Guide* (Headline, 1995). A useful and very readable review of the increasing medical evidence that moderate consumption of wine helps to prevent heart disease.

Larousse Encyclopedia of Wine (Larousse, 1994). Useful work of reference; more approachable than *The Oxford Companion to Wine* but less detailed.

ALEX LIDDELL AND JANET PRICE *Port Wine Quintas of the Douro* (Sothebys, 1992). Detailed and well-illustrated study of the Port estates in the Duoro.

JOHN LIVINGSTONE-LEARMONTH *The Wines of the Rhône* (Faber & Faber, 1992). The definitive guide to these wines and now in its 4th edition.

KERMIT LYNCH *Adventures on the Wine Trail* (Bodley Head, 1988). Lively and very readable account of Lynch's, an American wine merchant, wine-buying trips to France.

GILES MACDONOGH *Wine & Food of Austria* (Mitchell Beazley, 1992). The only book in English on Austrian wine.

RICHARD MAYSON *Portugal's Wines and Wine Makers* (Ebury Press, 1992). Detailed if rather dense guide to Portuguese wines.

REMINGTON NORMAN *The Great Domaines of Burgundy* (Kyle Cathie, 1992). Detailed study of the great estates of the Côte d'Or.

REMINGTON NORMAN *Rhône Renaissance 'The finest Rhône and Rhône-style wines from France and the New World* (Mitchell Beazley, 1995). This is a detailed study of those increasingly fashionable Rhône grapes and places them in a global context.

GEORGE ORDISH *The Great Wine Blight* (Sidgwick & Jackson, 1987). A fascinating account of phylloxera and the devastation it wrought in Europe at the end of the last century.

ROBERT PARKER *Wine Buyer's Guide* (Dorling Kindersley, 1995). Influential and controversial, Parker is best known, loved and loathed for his 100 point ratings.

EDMUND PENNING-ROWSELL *The Wines of Bordeaux* (6th edn, Penguin, 1989). Now in its 6th edition. Strongest on the history of Bordeaux's wine trade and those of the estates.

STUART PIGOTT *The Wine Atlas of Germany and Travellers Guide to the Vineyards* (Mitchell Beazley, 1995). Important new work from the controversial Pigott as the suggested classification of German's leading vineyards, first proposed in *Hugh Johnson's World Atlas of Wine* (4th Edition), are developed and refined.

DAVID PEPPERCORN *The Wines of Bordeaux* (Faber & Faber, 1991). Authoritative guide, now in its 2nd edition.

JOHN PLATTER'S *South African Wine Guide* (Mitchell Beazley, annually). Authoritative guide to the Republic's fast changing wines.

JANCIS ROBINSON *OUP Companion to Wine* (1994). Contains a remarkable amount of information, this is an indispensable reference book and well worth the money.

STEVEN SPURRIER *Guide to French Wines* (Mitchell Beazley, 1991). Although now becoming a little dated, this is a sound guide.

PAUL STRANG *The Wines of South-West France* (Kyle Cathie, 1994). Detailed account of little-known but fascinating wines such as Cahors, Madiran, and Irouléguy.

TOM STEVENSON *The Wines of Alsace* (Faber & Faber, 1993). A detailed, if overlong survey.

BOB THOMPSON *The Wine Atlas of California with Oregon and Washington* (Mitchell Beazley, 1993). Particularly useful for anyone intending to visit the West Coast vineyards, although curiously there is little mention of phylloxera, which is now having such an effect in California.

ROGER VOSS *The Wines of the Loire* (Faber & Faber, 1995). The Loire has been poorly served by English wine books, sadly although this new book is welcome it is not as detailed as it might be.

WINE COURSES, LECTURES, AND VACATIONS

Interest in wine continues to grow and there are an increasing number of courses run on wine and vacations based around the idea that it is fun to visit vineyards and meet the people who make the wine. All levels of interest are now catered for and here are some useful addresses.

LECTURES AND COURSES

In the United States contact:

WINE & SPIRIT EDUCATION CENTERS OF AMERICA INC., Frank H. Stone, PO Box 20450, Atlanta, Georgia 30325.

In France contact:

L'ECOLE DU VIN, Château Loudenne, St-Yzans du Médoc, 33340 Lesparre. Residential wine courses in Bordeaux's Médoc.

In Britain contact:

CHRISTIE'S WINE COURSES, 63 Old Brompton Road, London SW7 3JS, tel: 0171-581 3933.

THE CIRCLE OF WINE WRITERS booklet, called "Winespeak", gives details of members who lecture. Contact: Andrew Henderson, 94 Cavendish Road, London SW12 0DF, tel: 0181-675 2565.

MICHAEL SCHUSTER, 107 Culford Road, London N1 4HL, tel: 0171-254 9734

WINE AND SPIRIT EDUCATION TRUST, Five Kings House, 1 Queen Street Place, London EC4 1QS, tel: 0171-236 3551.

Also, a number of local authorities run wine appreciation classes.

VACATIONS

In the United States contact:

NAPA VALLEY BALLOONS INC., PO Box 2860, Yountville, CA 94599, tel: 707/944-0228 (800/253-2224 in California)

In Britain contact:

ARBLASTER & CLARKE, Freepost, Petersfield, GU32 2BD, tel: 01730-895344.

THE SUNDAY TIMES WINE TOURS, Freepost, Petersfield, GU32 2BD, tel: 01730-895353.

TANGLEWOOD WINE TOURS, Mayfield Ave, New Haw, Surrey KT15 3AG, tel: 01932-348720.

WINE TRAILS, Greenways, Vann Lake, Ockley, Dorking RH5 5NT, tel: 01306-712111.

Interested in buying a share in a French Vineyard? Contact David Dickinson, 3D Wines, Holly Lodge, High Street, Swineshead, Lincolnshire PE20 3LH, tel: 01205-820745.

APPELLATION CONTRÔLÉE: The top category of French wine which is intended to guarantee the geographical authenticity of the wine. Unfortunately, it does not always guarantee its quality.

AVA: Californian appellation system based on geography.

AUSBRUCH: Austrian term for a wine between Beerenauslese and Trockenbeerenauslese.

BOTTLE FERMENTED: (*méthode traditionelle* or *méthode champenoise*): the secondary fermentation took place in the bottle. All of the best sparkling wines are made this way.

BRUT: a dry sparkling wine with up to 15 grams of sugar per liter.

BRUT ZERO: a sparkling wine with no, or very little, sugar added at dosage stage.

CAVA: term for Spanish bottle fermented wine.

COSECHA: Spanish for vintage.

CRÉMANT: joint term used by seven sparkling wine appellations in France plus Luxembourg, which have the same strict rules as Champagne.

CRIANZA: Spanish term for a wine that has been aged but for not long enough to qualify as a reserva.

CUVÉE: a very imprecise term, as in Cuvée Reservée, which just means blend.

DEMI-SEC: semi-sweet

DO (Spain): means Denominación de Origen and is similar to the French AC system.

DOC (meaning Denominazione di Origine Controllata): Italian appellation system that is meaningless because there are far too many designated areas. Supposed to be the process of reform.

DOC: On a bottle of Portuguese wine, this is the top regional classification.

DOCG (meaning Denominazione di Origine Controllata e Garantita): Italy's top wine category, only eight wines have this honor.

EISWEIN: Made from grapes picked during a hard frost, usually at the end of December or beginning of January. The grapes are quickly pressed while they are still frozen. The juice is concentrated because the frozen water content is left behind.

ELÈVÉ EN FUTS DE CHÊNE: aged in oak barrels.

GRAND CRU: The vineyards of Burgundy have a very detailed classification system, which assesses the quality of every vineyard. The very best such as Corton, Montrachet, Romanée-Conti are classified as Grand Cru. The local villages have added the name of the vineyards to their own to increase their status as in Aloxe-Corton. Alsace also has its best sites classified as Grand Cru and used for the third tier of châteaux in St. Emilion.

GRAND CRU CLASSÉ: Refers to the top properties in the Médoc, St. Emilion, and Sauternes.

GRAN RESERVA (Spain): Two years in wood, followed by three years in bottle.

GARRAFEIRA: Portuguese term for an extremely good vintage. Garrafeiras are aged for two years in wood, followed by a year in bottle for reds and six months for whites.

LATE HARVEST: grapes picked after the rest of the harvest. The wine is often, but not invariably, sweet.

MÉTHODE CHAMPENOISE: French term for sparkling wine made using secondary fermentation in bottle. After a long campaign by the Champagne producers, term is now banned in Europe. Hypocritically, some Champagne houses still use the term in California to describe their sparkling wines.

MISE EN BOUTEILLE: French for bottled. This expression is often found on bottles of French wine to show who did the bottling.

MOELLEUX: sweet. Mainly used on wines from the Loire and parts of southwest France.

PASSITO (Italy): A sweet wine that has been made from grapes that have been laid out to dry and so concentrate their juice. The French call these wines *vin de paille*.

PREMIER CRU: The second-ranked Burgundian vineyards, one up from straight village. But confusingly in Bordeaux the top classification.

Q.B A (Germany): stands for *Qualitätswein bestimmter Anbaugebiete*. This is Germany's middle quality wine and from a designated area. Sugar may be added to the must before fermentation.

QUALITÄTSWEIN MIT PRADIKAT (QMP) (Germany): This is the top category for German wines, into which sugar may not be added. Producers have to rely instead on the grape's natural ripeness. The terms Kabinett, Spätlese (late picked), Auslese (very ripe grapes often with some noble rot), Beerenauslese (selected very ripe grapes, often with noble rot), and Trockenbeerenauslese (extremely ripe, nobly rotted grapes) indicate the sweetness of the wine. Austria uses a similar classification.

RESERVA (Spain): One year in wood, then two in bottle.

RISERVA (Italy): Wine aged for a specified period. The required length of time varies from region to region.

SEC: French for dry. Often found on bottles from the Loire and parts of southwest France where they make dry and sweet versions of the same wine. In sparkling wines not as dry as brut.

SELECTION DE GRAINS NOBLES: grapes with noble rot, used especially in Alsace and increasingly in Coteaux du Layon.

TAFELWEIN (Germany): Table wine.

VENDANGE TARDIVE: Late harvest, used especially in Alsace.

VIEILLES VIGNES: French for old vines. Mature vines give more concentrated juice and should make more interesting wines. But there is no agreement on what age a vine becomes old.

VQA: Quality seal for Canadian wine and means Vintner Quality Alliance.

VINO DA TAVOLA (Italy): Table wine. Confusingly this includes some of Italy's cheapest and most expensive wines.

VIN DE PAYS: French term for country wine, a step up from vin de table. Now a very important category especially in the south of France and, in particular, for varietal wines.

VINTAGE: Because the climate is always variable, vintages are very important. This is particularly true in cool climate areas such as Northern Europe and New Zealand. However, even in California and Australia there are marked variations from one year to another. Most wine carries a vintage date irrespective of how good or poor the year was. Only champagne and port actually declare a vintage and then only in good years as the bulk of their production is sold without a vintage date.

ACKNOWLEDGEMENTS

THE PUBLISHERS THANK the contributors of photographs: Jim Budd: p. 11, 12, 14, 27–33, 36, 39–46, 48, 49, 52, 53, 55, 58, 59, 74, 78, 79, 88, 89, 100, 101, 109, 120, 125, 126, 130; Centre One Advertising & Marketing Ltd.: p. 13; Kevin Argue: p. 29; Chris Davis: p 132; Rick England: p. 146; Juan Espi: p. 136; Kevin Judd: p. 65, Alain Proust: p. 17, 20, 136, 137; John Rizzo: p. 65; Mick Rock: p. 30, 45, 51, 61–3, 70, 105, 109, 127–9, 139–141, 144, 146 – of Cephas Picture Library; Andrew Jefford: p. 131; Janet Price: 27, 32, 34, 36–41, 68, 69, 78, 92, 93, 114, 117, 122, 127, 132, 149–152; Texas Department of Transportation: p. 60; and thanks go to Christine Sloan for map illustrations; and to the following suppliers for items for photography: Broadstone Communications (Richmond, Surrey TW9 1EU); Rosalia Vergaras of Bibendum (London, NW1 8UR); E. Herzog and R. P. Brown of Oddbins; J. Jey of Thresher (Clapham Junction, London); Tetra Pak UK (Uxbridge, Middx. UB11 1DL); and Safeways Wine Stores.

GREENLAND

CANADA

U.S.A

CALIFORNIA

SAN
FRANCISCO

LOS
ANGELES

NEW
YORK

BRITISH
ISLES

GERMANY

FRANCE

SPAIN

PORTUGAL

Atlantic Ocean

Pacific
Ocean

SOUTH
AMERICA

CHILE

SANTIAGO

A